dreamfinder

DISCOVERING THE DIVINE / THROUGH YOUR DREAMS

Dream

DISCOVERING THE DIVINE   THROUGH YOUR DREAMS

PHILIP DUNN AND SANGEET DUCHANE

**Andrews McMeel
Publishing**

Kansas City

Andrews McMeel Publishing
an Andrews McMeel Universal company
4520 Main Street
Kansas City, Missouri 64111

04 05 06 07 08 RR2 10 9 8 7 6 5 4 3 2 1

ISBN: 0-7407-4175-6

Library of Congress Control Number: 2004044871

Cover Art: *Flaming June* by Lord Frederic Leighton

Design by Amy Ray

Contents

What's in a Dream?

This book is designed to help you find the key to understanding the incredible world of your dreams. By unlocking your dreams, you can open up a vast reservoir of information that you might not yet be aware of; information that your unconscious brings you every night. If you sleep eight hours a night, you sleep ten days out of every month. In an average lifetime a person sleeps for about twenty-five years. During that time you have an average of five or more dreams every night, even if you can't remember them. The time you spend sleeping is not just downtime useful only to rejuvenate you. It's a time of intense creativity, and your dreams contain a gold mine of information for your life, your health, and your spiritual development.

Sometimes we think of dreams as not real or less real than our waking state. "It was only a dream," we say. But for people of ancient times and for aboriginal people today, there was and is no such distinction

between dreams and "reality." These people believe that dreams provide them with important information and sometimes even allow them to speak directly to God or other supernatural entities. According to legend, the whole course of history was changed in the fourth century B.C.E., when the Roman Emperor Constantine had a dream on the eve of a major battle. He dreamed that Jesus was telling him to put the monogram of Christ on the shields of his soldiers. He did that and won the battle. As a result of the victory, Constantine legalized Christianity and eventually made it the official religion of the empire. This change, which has affected the entire development of Western civilization, happened because Constantine believed that his dream was a real message from Jesus.

We are becoming more aware that our dreams are real in that they give us a means of self-exploration, access to important information, and insights into what we should do and what may happen in the future. And best of all, this exploration can be a lot of fun. The word *dream* comes from the Middle English word *dreem*, which means "joy" and "music." This book is a guide to having fun while you realize the full potential of your dreams.

DREAMS IN ANCIENT TIMES

There are clay tablets dating back as far as 3000 to 4000 B.C.E. that discuss dream interpretation. If those ancient people took the trouble to record that information, it must have been important to them. In Egypt the priests were the interpreters of dreams, and dreams were sometimes recorded in hieroglyphs. People who had vivid and significant dreams were seen as gifted and special. In the Greek and Roman cultures dream interpreters would accompany the military leaders into battle, where dreams, such as the one Constantine had, were considered extremely important.

The ancients not only believed that dreams contained important information but also thought that dreams foretold the future. There are over seven hundred references to dreams in the Bible, many of them related to biblical prophecy. In other cultures, dreams dictated the course of politics and government as well as plans for individual lives.

Ancient people also used dreams for healing. In some cases the patient would dream and the healer would interpret the dream to determine the best course of treatment. In other cases the healer would dream and receive information needed to effect a cure.

dreamfinder

In ancient times there was no theory of the conscious or unconscious mind to explain dreams; people believed that dreams were actual communications from another realm: from God, a variety of gods, demons, nature, or ancestors. These were messages that they couldn't afford to ignore, for fear of offending the messengers or of bringing bad fortune on themselves.

In the European Age of Enlightenment, when science began to replace what was called superstition, dreams were disregarded, along with belief in gods and demons and messages from beyond. Many people came to see dreams as nothing more than the results of physical discomfort or maybe indigestion. This perspective changed with the late nineteenth- and early twentieth-century work of Sigmund Freud and his contemporaries, though the psychological interpretations that followed tended to see dreams in terms of only the mental processes of the individual dreamer. As we will see, this theory of the purely psychological origin of dreams isn't really sufficient to explain all the information people receive or experiences they have in their dreams.

WHAT WILL YOUR DREAMS TELL YOU?

Why pay attention to what you are dreaming? Because your dreams have a lot of very valuable information to give you. Your dreams bring you information you don't usually have access to in your day-to-day life.

Insights into Something You Aren't Seeing

Your dreams can tell you things about your life you aren't consciously aware of or that you don't want to see. Your unconscious mind records everything, even things that you don't consciously notice. Your conscious mind can hold only so much information at a time, but information isn't lost; it just goes into the unconscious. So, for example, your unconscious mind records what you have done and can remember where you "lost" something, even if you have consciously forgotten where you put it. Your unconscious mind will also record all your emotions and the body language of everyone around you. So if your new lover is giving you signals that he's unreliable, you will know it unconsciously, even if you've been trying to convince yourself that he's the one. You'll know if you need to change your job, even if you're too worried about the job market to consider changes.

11

dreamfinder

You might dream of being chased, of violence, or of some other danger if you are worried about some unresolved issue. You might dream of being involved in a conflict when you are torn inside about something. Dreams give you insight into yourself and insight into your relationships. If you dream that you can fly but someone keeps holding you down, that person, or whomever the person in the dream represents to you, may be holding you down in some psychological or energetic way.

Nightmares, especially recurring nightmares, can give you important insights into where your anxieties lie or what incidents in your life are unresolved. In this and all other circumstances, your dreams are an incredible gift, allowing you to access the resources of your unconscious mind. In dreams you are able to sort through the information you couldn't take in consciously while you were awake and to draw important lessons from it. You are able to see things that you might resist or not want to see but that are important for you to know.

Information from Beyond the Individual Unconscious

Sometimes you get information in dreams that you have no way of knowing, even from the observation of your unconscious mind. In the nineteenth century Dmitry Mendeleyev presented the world with the periodic table of elements after seeing it in a dream. People have also dreamed how to resolve a nagging physical complaint. Where does this information come from?

There are a variety of explanations, of course. The psychic Edgar Cayce spoke of the Akashic records or Book of Life, where he said all the information about everyone who has ever lived on Earth is stored. Cayce used this information in his trances to give advice about healing. On one occasion he told a pharmacist exactly where an old bottle of herbal remedy, which the pharmacist didn't even know existed, was stored. Cayce said that others can access the Akashic records too.

Helena Petrovna Blavatsky, the nineteenth-century theosophist and mystic, also spoke about the principle of Akasha in her book *Alchemy and the Secret Doctrine.* "Akasha is one of the cosmic principles and is a plastic matter, creative in its physical nature, immutable in its higher principles. It is the quintessence of all possible forms of energy, material, psychic, or spiritual; and contains within itself the germs of universal creation, which sprout forth under the impulse of the Divine Spirit."

Rudolph Steiner, the late nineteenth-century and early twentieth-century Austrian philosopher, educator, and founder of the Anthroposophical Society, could perceive information in a spiritual world that was as real to him as the physical world. This is the way ancient people and contemporary aboriginal people tend to experience dreams, as another, equally real reality, where information is available for the asking.

Perhaps this is the source of the information in the dream state, but whatever the source, there is no question that incredible amounts of information are available. This information is often very basic and practical. For example, a real estate agent with a difficult client once dreamed of the perfect property, one he had never heard of. When the agent tracked it down, the property was just what the client was looking for, and he bought it. Information about business, employment, relationships, places to live, and other day-to-day issues may all be available to you in your dreams.

14

Access to Your Creativity

The dream state seems to be a particularly good place to get in touch with creative potential. Inventors, composers, dancers, poets, and many other highly creative people attribute some of their finest work to inspiration from their dreams. Paul McCartney's song "Yesterday," Samuel Taylor Coleridge's poem "Kubla Khan," and Robert Louis Stevenson's novel *The Strange Case of Dr. Jekyll and Mr. Hyde* are just a few examples. Other dream-inspired artists include Mozart, Beethoven, William Blake, Paul Klee, and Ingmar Bergman.

Your dreams can tell you the best outlet for your creativity and can provide a space where that creativity can flow unchecked by conscious evaluation or criticism. Creative information such as designs, story lines, and images may be presented to you regularly. The only question is whether you are paying enough attention to benefit from these gifts.

Rehearsal of Physical and Professional Skills

The psychologist Paul Tholey used dream work to help train the German Olympic ski-jumping team. Team members learned how to direct their dreams (see

Chapter 3) to try out new maneuvers. Now some coaches are using similar techniques to improve business and professional performance. This kind of information isn't available only in controlled dreams. The golfer Jack Nicklaus has told how he got out of a slump with just one spontaneous dream that corrected an error he had been making in his swing.

It's probable that small children practice and perfect new motor skills in their dreams and that older people who are learning new skills like skateboarding, driving, or skiing also practice and perfect those skills in their dreams, whether they are aware of doing so or not.

Healing Advice

Dreams can reveal important information about the physical body, perhaps because the body is recording symptoms the conscious mind hasn't noticed. Dreams can tell you when to go to the doctor or dentist, which doctor is right for you, what treatment option to choose, where to find new treatment options, and sometimes even about unknown or unusual treatments.

Predictions of the Future

The ancients thought that dreams foretold the future, and many modern people agree with them. It is reported that a short time before he was assassinated Abraham Lincoln dreamed he was at a funeral. When he asked a soldier who was in the casket, the soldier said it was the president of the United States. Mark Twain dreamed of seeing his brother in a coffin. A week later his brother was killed, and when Twain arrived for the funeral, he saw his brother's body, just as it had been in his dream. In 1914 the Catholic Bishop Joseph Lanyl dreamed that the Archduke of Austria, Francis Ferdinand de Hapsburg, would be assassinated. He tried in vain to reach the archduke, who was killed on June 28, 1914, triggering the start of World War I.

Sometimes people change their minds about doing something or take precautions because of a dream and manage to avoid a disaster. After the sinking of the *Titanic*, at least two dozen people claimed to have canceled their reservations because of dreams. One woman passenger dreamed that the ship would sink the day before it happened. She had her children sleep in their clothes, and they were able to get to the lifeboats and survive. We will never know how many others

17

onboard had similar dreams and ignored them. Some people have dreamed of getting lung cancer and stopped smoking; others have taken precautions to prevent an accident that would have happened just as they dreamed it had they not known about it in advance. Possibly none of us can afford to forget or disregard this kind of dream.

Visits from Beyond

We have probably all dreamed about a loved one who died or talked to someone who has. This kind of dream is very understandable as a part of the grieving process, but sometimes these dreams seem so real that the dreamer is convinced that a visit actually happened. These visits often involve a message that the departed one is fine and happy or that there is something the living person needs to do. Sometimes these appearances also warn of danger.

When the message is that the departed loved one is fine, the dreamer is often so relieved that the grieving process is eased. This dramatic result makes it even more convincing that the visit was real.

People also experience dream visits from spiritual guides that they may call angels, saints, or teachers.

These visitations are powerfully affecting. The visitor may offer guidance on any subject—health, work, relationship, or spiritual development. Or the guide may appear as someone who is protecting the dreamer, giving the message that help is near.

Celebration of Growth and Illumination

Dreams can be a way to celebrate joy in life, your expansion, and your growth. Flying dreams, fun-filled dreams, and dreams of exploration, like finding a new room in an old house or discovering a new place, can all represent your acknowledgment of your growth and learning. Or they can be reminders to celebrate and appreciate these events. You might also have a dream in which you are unexpectedly appreciated and supported by others, maybe someone very unlikely. This may be a way of telling you that you have achieved more than you realize.

Out-of-Body Experiences

Another dream experience is moving out of the body, sometimes looking down at your body on your bed, then moving on to some other location. The sensation of leaving the body is often preceded by a loud noise. This is a surprisingly common experience; some researchers claim that from 5 to 35 percent of people have had an out-of-body experience at some time.

There is a lot of debate about whether people having these dreams actually travel to another location in the physical world or move into some other realm. Those who think people are moving to another physical place sometimes argue that the soul is separating from the body and traveling in the physical world. Others argue that the spirit travels into another dimension. Some people think both things happen.

We have never disregarded the possibility that people are really traveling to another physical location since the time we heard this story. When a friend of ours was a boy, he used to travel out of body fairly frequently. Doing so was easy for him, and he didn't think it was strange. One day he left his body and was hovering over an intersection in the town where he lived. Suddenly there was a terrible automobile accident in which some people were killed. He felt the sensation of terrified people passing through him as they rose out of the cars below. He snapped back into his body and was so shocked that his parents rushed him to the emergency room, not knowing what was wrong. He arrived at the hospital at the same time as the ambulances bringing survivors from the accident he had witnessed. He was so disturbed by the experience that he never consciously traveled out of body again. Still, there is no doubt that he left the confines of his physical body and went to a very real location, where he encountered an event taking place in our shared physical reality.

There are also many stories of yogis and other esoteric practitioners who can travel out of body at will. Some of these practitioners have reportedly been seen as physical presences in different places at the same time. Many things are possible, and it will be up to each dreamer to decide if an out-of-body experience was a journey in the physical realm or into another realm.

Dream researchers have found that out-of-body experiences usually occur in REM sleep, when the body is effectively paralyzed. Some argue that the sensation of separating from the body is just the sleeper's awareness that the body can't move. This feeling of paralysis, however, doesn't prove that out-of-body experiences don't really happen. They may simply happen more easily when the body is immobilized.

It is interesting that some people report out-of-body experiences while in engaged in daily activity, like walking down the street, so out-of-body experiences aren't limited to times when the body is in a state of paralysis.

All of this tells us that dream information is important and worth listening to. In some cases the information we receive may be a matter of life and death. Dream experiences may also give us access to sources of information we have not yet imagined.

[The pages at the end of each chapter give you an opportunity to record important information about your own dreams that relate to the chapter.]

MY DREAMS FROM BEYOND:
DREAMS I FEEL I CANNOT FATHOM

Dreams and Spiritual Practice

Many of the world's religious traditions have recognized the importance of dreams. Dreams may be a time to commune with a deity, a time for inner search, or a time to engage in spiritual practices.

DREAMING IN EASTERN TRADITIONS

Several Eastern spiritual traditions have developed methods of using dreams or the dream state as a part of spiritual practice. These practices often employ what are called lucid dreaming techniques, which means you are conscious that you are dreaming during the dream itself. Chapter 3 will cover this subject in more detail.

Tibetan Buddhism

Tibetan practitioners employ what is often called dream yoga, a discipline of using dreams to become more aware of the illusionary nature of all reality. Tibetan dream yoga separates dreams into three major

categories. The first includes ordinary dreams brought about by the day's concerns or by past experience and proclivities. These are also called karma. The second category is "clear light" dreams, which may include spiritual teachings, visions, healing, and vital energy openings. The last category is lucid dreaming, in which you can continue your spiritual practice, grow in awareness of life-change states, and prepare for death and dying.

The Tibetan dream yoga system also categorizes dreams into those about events that occurred while you were still awake but that need more attention; "message" dreams, in which you receive messages from people alive or dead; dreams showing forgotten parts of your psyche emerging into consciousness; symbolic dreams and dreams with archetypal content; dreams that contain precognitive elements, omens, or warnings, or are in some way extrasensory; and radiant dreams of great spiritual teaching or blessing.

Tibetan practice can also involve messages or visits from great masters. In his book *Dream Yoga and the Practice of Natural Light*, Namkhai Norbu tells of meeting various teachers, living and dead, being instructed in secret practices, and being shown secret texts known as "dream treasures." In one dream, while visiting the site of ancient ruins near Mount Kailash in Tibet, Norbu dreamed of reaching into a hole in the earth and extracting a valuable metal sculpture of a garuda—the ancient Indian mythological figure that is part eagle and part human. While breaking camp after he had awakened, Norbu thought he recognized a part of the landscape from his dream. Taking a closer look, he discovered a hole in the ground, and after considerable digging he unearthed a metal garuda just like the one in his dream.

Tibetan practitioners report visits from various teachers; sometimes these are historical teachers and sometimes they are other kinds of entities. The masters may give teachings or initiations into a spiritual practice or interact with the dreamer in some other way.

Hinduism

According to Hindu mythology, this world is the dream of the god Vishnu. As a result, what we think of as the physical world can be seen as a dream, and dreams can be seen as just another manifestation of *maya* or illusion. A Hindu scripture, the *Bhagavata Purana*, says, "Even though apparently awake, one is still

asleep if one sees multiplicity. Wake up from the dream of ignorance and see the one Self. The Self alone is real." Another scripture, the *Yoga Vasistha*, describes dreaming sleep as an opportunity for human beings to create as the gods create, by sending forth images. The *Brihadaranyaka Upanishad* describes the dream world this way: "In that land there are no lakes, no lotus-ponds, nor streams; but [the Spirit of humanity] creates its own lakes, its lotus-ponds, and streams. For the Spirit of humanity is Creator."

Sufism

The interpretation of dreams, including dreams that involve dialogues with one's teachers, have formed an important aspect of some Sufi orders since their earliest days. Najd ad-din Kubra (1145–1220) worked extensively with dream interpretation. He recommended the "constant direction of a shaykh who explains the meanings of one's dreams and visions." In other words, he believed that dreams are tools for the spiritual master or teacher to use in helping the student move along the spiritual path. Baha ad-din Naqshband of Bukhara (d. 1389), founder of the Naqshbandi Order of Sufism, was well known as an interpreter of dreams.

DREAMS AND SPIRITUAL PRACTICE

It is said that Naqshband would not accept a dervish or disciple until he had a dream indicating that the candidate was an appropriate disciple. So he was guided by his own dreams as well as working with the dreams of his disciples.

Taoism

Taoist practitioners emphasize the paradoxical and interdependent nature of dreaming and what we usually call reality. The fourth century B.C.E. Taoist sage, Chuang-tzu, is famous for wondering whether he was a butterfly dreaming he was Chuang-tzu or Chuang-tzu dreaming he was a butterfly. He concluded that all was a dream:

"He who dreams of drinking wine may weep when morning comes; he who dreams of weeping may in the morning go off to hunt. While he is dreaming he does not know it is a dream, and in his dream he may even try to interpret a dream. Only after he wakes does he know it was a dream. And someday there will be a great awakening when we know that this is all a great dream. Yet the stupid believe they are awake, busily and brightly assuming they understand things, calling this man ruler, that one herdsman—how dense! Confucius and you are both dreaming! And when I say you are dreaming, I am dreaming too."

Taoism contains specific techniques for dream yoga. Taoist dream practice, called true dream, dream wandering, or night practice, uses sleep and dream as a form of meditation. Sleep is seen as a natural time for the practice of meditation. The prerequisite for any dream work is sufficient sound sleep, achieved through rest, exercise, proper eating, and an occasional nap. The first level of practice is to establish healthy and harmonious sleep. After that the practitioner begins to discover the dream body, which is the vehicle for meditation and exploration.

DREAM MEDITATIONS

Because the period of time between the waking state and sleep is one of transition from the conscious to the unconscious, it is a time when meditation can be very powerful. Several meditation techniques have been developed to make use of those precious moments. Many mystics have taught that the thought we take into sleep is the one that will stay with us throughout the night. Gautama Buddha, for example, had his disciples meditate for an hour before falling asleep so that they would go into sleep in a meditative state.

Several specific meditation techniques can be used to release the tensions of the day and fall into a meditative sleep. One way is simply to tune in as you lie in bed and release the thoughts and tensions that are left over from your day. You can unwind the day to the beginning and complete for yourself anything that feels incomplete. Such conscious completion can leave you free for a meditative dreamtime. This technique is not remembering or standing aloof; it involves actually reliving the situations as though you were in them.

Another meditation technique to lead into sleep is to turn off the lights and sit in your bed. Allow your body to relax and to move into any position it wants. If it wants to lie flat on your back, allow it. If it wants to curl up in a fetal position, allow it. Once the body has taken a position, just listen to your breath. No need to do anything or think about anything. Simply listen to your breath as you fall asleep.

If you want to sit in meditation before sleeping, it's best to finish all your preparations for bed before you start to meditate, so that you can go directly to bed and fall asleep while you are still in the space of meditation.

Meditation is often enhanced and supported by involving the senses of hearing and smell, with music or incense or essential oils. If you have particular music or a special scent that you associate with meditation, use it as you fall asleep to give a cue to your unconscious mind that it is time for meditation.

If your sleep is being disturbed, if you are waking up tense, or if you are having nightmares, it might help to do a cathartic release meditation before you go to bed. In this way you let go of tensions before you sleep and leave the sleep time free for rest, relaxation, and meditation. One technique for releasing tension is to turn off the light and sit on your bed. Imagine that you are a three-year-old child, and allow yourself to move and make noises. Don't speak in words, since they may get you thinking and analyzing. The point is to release tension without thinking about it. If you want to cry, cry. If you want to laugh, laugh. Just be innocent and childlike again. As you begin to feel tired, in that same innocence, fall asleep. In a short time you should find yourself sleeping much more deeply.

The last technique is a death and life meditation. This meditation is a relaxation into both, reinforcing the idea that life and death are part of the same cycle.

Before you go to sleep, turn off the lights and close your eyes. Imagine that you are dead. Feel that you can't move your body at all. Imagine yourself disappearing from your body. If you want, imagine yourself in a coffin or grave. Relax. Maintain this visualization for ten to fifteen minutes, then fall asleep.

In the morning when you wake up, keep your eyes closed. Begin to move and feel alive. Feel the life and vitality flowing through your body. Take deep breaths as you experience this life in you.

As you continue to do this meditation at night and in the morning, you begin to feel the rhythm of life and death and understand that death is nothing to be afraid of. When you understand this, you can truly be alive for the first time.

Try these meditations or others that you may learn from books or teachers. The important thing to remember is that the thought or mental state you take into your sleep will guide your dreams. If you take tension into your sleep, your dreams will be about releasing tension. If you take a question into your sleep, your dreams will be about your question. If you take meditation into your sleep, your dreams will be meditations.

SECRET DREAMS DREAMS

Creating Dreams

The first step in advanced dream techniques is to become conscious enough in your dreams to direct their course. This is called lucid dreaming.

LUCID DREAMING THROUGH THE AGES

Reports of lucid dreaming go back far further than Aristotle. If we are to believe the Tibetan Bonpo School of dream masters, their founder, Tonpa Shenrab, lived over fifteen millennia ago. The oral traditions of the Vedantic and Upanishadic texts of India are believed to have existed five thousand years ago, while the Jaina traditions claim even greater antiquity. Traditions have varied on how to induce or invoke lucid dreaming, but all appear to regard being conscious while dreaming as a prerequisite for any spiritual path.

The clearest writings on the subject is found in an ancient tantric text, the *Vigyan Bhairav Tantra*, one of

the treasures of the Hindu world. These are the 112 meditation techniques given to his consort, Devi, by Lord Shiva. *Vigyan* can be roughly translated as consciousness, *bhairav* refers to one who has gone beyond, and *tantra* is the method.

Two thousand five hundred years ago, one of the Buddha's greatest disciples was Sariputta. We are told in texts of the time that as his meditations deepened, he began to experience many strange visions and lucid dreams. They were so perfectly actualized that he insisted they were as real as the Buddha himself.

What must have been a golden age of lucidity came between the eighth and twelfth centuries of the Common Era in Tibet. Some of the greatest Buddhist mystics ever known conceived and wrote the *Tibetan Book of the Dead*. They created an experientially based science of lucid dreaming, which our scientific age is only beginning to recognize as being in advance of anything we know of.

The earliest Western reference to lucid dreaming appears to be in a letter written by Saint Augustine in the fourth century. Augustine was quoting an earlier dream of a physician from Carthage, one Gennadius, in which a youth of "remarkable appearance and commanding presence" interrogated him. In a subsequent sequence of nightly dreams, the youth quizzed him on the nature and state of his dreaming. Gennadius was asked whether these events had taken place in sleep or wakefulness. When he replied that he knew he was still sleeping, the youth reminded him that even so he was seeing in his sleep. This declaration startled the dreamer into waking up within his dream.

The youth continued his inquisition. "Where is your body now?" To which Gennadius replied that it was in his bed. "Do you know that the cells in this body of yours are bound and closed, and that with these eyes you are seeing nothing?" questioned the youth. "As while you are asleep and lying on your bed these eyes of your body are now unemployed and doing nothing, and yet you have eyes with which you behold me, and enjoy this vision, so, after your death, while your bodily eyes shall be wholly inactive there shall be in you a life by which you shall live, and a faculty of perception by which you shall perceive." This message is as heartening for us to hear today as it was, no doubt, for Saint Augustine.

While Persian Sufis were practicing spectacular telepathic and shared lucid dreams, the twelfth-century

Sufi Elc Arabi asserted that disciples should learn to coordinate thoughts in a dream.

The thirteenth-century Christian theologian Thomas Aquinas gave a rare and valuable clue as to when a conscious dream would be most likely. He said that lucidity most commonly occurs "towards the end of sleep, in sober men and those gifted with strong imaginations."

Although there were a number of isolated cases of lucid dreamers, few seem to have survived the lean years from the fourteenth through the eighteenth centuries. This scarcity was probably the result of a combination of the zeal of the Spanish Inquisition on the one hand and the new Age of Reason on the other.

So it was not until the middle of the nineteenth century that a real dream pioneer described his experiences in the fascinating volume *Dreams and How to Guide Them*. This was the first methodical examination of lucidity in dreams, written by the Marquis d'Hervey de Saint-Denys. He recounted how he had learned to recall, awaken in, and control his dreams in a journal that documented twenty years of careful research. But his work was received with skepticism by the scientific community of the time.

Even when the famous philosopher Friedrich Nietzsche made an obvious reference to his lucid dreams, saying, "And perhaps many a one will, like myself, recollect having sometimes called out cheeringly and not without success amid the dangers and terrors of dream life: 'It is a dream! I will dream on!'" Few rallied to explore such phenomena.

Sigmund Freud, the pioneer of Western therapeutic dream work, did not mention lucid dreaming at all in the first edition of his mammoth *Interpretation of Dreams*. He did, however, add a small footnote to the second edition in which he briefly acknowledged that "there are some people who are quite clearly aware during the night that they are asleep and dreaming and who thus seem to possess the faculty of consciously directing their dreams. If, for instance, a dreamer of this kind is dissatisfied with the turn taken by a dream, he can break it off without warning and start again in another direction—just as a popular dramatist may under pressure give his play a happier ending."

Frederik Willem van Eeden, well known and respected in Holland, was the first one to coin the phrase "lucid dreaming," and the first to systematically research the state of being asleep, especially that

dreaming state which included a full recollection of daily life, awareness of the sleeping self, and the ability to act voluntarily within the dream.

TECHNIQUES FOR LUCID DREAMING

Lucid or conscious dreaming is a technique with tremendous potential for the adventurous dreamer. This technique has been used by shamans or "travelers between worlds" to visit the realms of the spirits in order to gain healing power and insight for both themselves and their people. In the East this form of dreaming has long been recognized as a method of achieving spiritual freedom. The ultimate object of this practice is to wake up rather than to get lost in an even greater labyrinth of dreams. There are methods available to everyone that allow a glimpse of what the sages talk about, and this is the phenomenon of lucid conscious dreaming.

Entering a Lucid Dream

The first task for a lucid dreamer is to create, or incubate, a lucid dream. People have found several ways to do this, and you might develop techniques of your own. Here are three possible ways.

One technique is to determine a question, a topic, a place you want to visit, or an action you want to carry out. Express it in the form of one question or phrase that you write down. If you are a visual person, draw a picture. Underneath your phrase or picture, write something like "When I dream [fill in phrase], I will remember that I am dreaming." For example, "When I dream I am walking, I will remember that I am dreaming."

Go to bed immediately. Make sure you've completed all your preparations for bed before you start this process. As you begin to fall asleep, focus on your phrase or picture. Also focus on your intention to be conscious in the dream. If your mind begins to wander, gently bring it back to your phrase or picture until you fall asleep.

A similar approach is to ask for a lucid dream but not specify one. To do this, simply focus on a sentence like "I will have a lucid dream, and I will remember it" as you fall asleep. Again, if your mind begins to wander, gently bring it back to this thought.

Experiments have shown that most lucid dreams happen in the last stages of REM (rapid eye movement) sleep. This discovery gave researchers the idea

that it might be easier to incubate lucid dreams if the dreamer got up before the usual time and went back to bed later for a nap. The results were remarkable, with the most success when a dreamer woke up two hours early, waited two hours—sometimes focusing on the idea of lucid dreaming or reading about it—then went back to bed for a two-hour nap. This technique produced ten times more lucid dreams than were created in normal sleep hours.

If you have difficulty incubating lucid dreams in your normal sleep hours and you have a flexible enough schedule, try this technique. You might also use it when you have a particularly important issue to address.

Another technique is related to the methods for reentering dreams. Tell yourself to wake up whenever you are dreaming and to remember your dream. You can say something like "I'll wake up whenever I'm dreaming, and I'll remember my dream." As with the other techniques, focus on this statement as you fall asleep and gently bring your mind back to it if you drift.

When you wake up, you can rouse yourself enough to record your dream. The lucid dream incubation technique is to relax again and imagine yourself back in the dream, but this time conscious that you're having a dream.

Determining Whether You Are Dreaming

As we said before, it isn't always easy to know when you're dreaming. To help you decide, you can use what are called "dream signs." For example, if you can do "impossible" things, like flying, you are in a dream. If you are in doubt, push off from the floor or bed with the intention of flying. If you can fly, you might want to head for the window and take off on a dream adventure. Another clue that you're dreaming is that people or things seem deformed or change shape or character. Or you might find yourself in a place you don't recognize.

Your dreams are uniquely yours, and so are your dream signs. It might help you to make a list of the things you have remembered in dreams that gave you the clue that you were dreaming. You can then use these signs to reinforce your lucid dream incubation. For example, if people often change to other people in your dreams, you can tell yourself that whenever a character changes you will become conscious that you are dreaming but won't wake up. If you have recurring events in your dreams, such as being chased by Nazis, you can tell yourself that every time you find yourself being chased by Nazis you will know you are dreaming and will become conscious in your dream.

Staying in a Lucid Dream

Many people, particularly those new to this practice, have trouble staying in a lucid dream. When they realize they are dreaming, they start to wake up. Several techniques have been developed to help the dreamer stay in the dream. The one most often used is spinning, which means twirling around in the dream body. This seems to focus attention on the dream body and stabilize the dream.

Looking at parts of the body, like the hands, or doing something like rubbing the hands together also gets the dreamer to focus on the dream body. You can use these techniques when you feel the dream is beginning to fade.

Reentering a Dream

If the techniques for staying in a dream don't work for you, all is not lost. You can reenter your dream by focusing on it as you fall back asleep, as we described before. Or use a self-hypnosis counting technique. For example, "One, I'm dreaming. Two, I'm dreaming…" or "One, I'm back in the dream. Two, I'm back in the dream…" Continue counting until you fall asleep.

Another technique is to focus on specific points on your body as you fall asleep. This method is intended to help you keep a conscious focus as you fall into sleep. The opposite approach also seems to work. Simply play dead. Stay relaxed and still and allow yourself to sink back into sleep without focusing on thoughts.

Using Dream Tasks

Some people use dream tasks to experiment with lucid dreams. You can create your own tasks. Here are a few that other people have developed.

In the light switch task, you find an indoor light switch and turn it on and off. Does the light level change? Now, instead of flipping the switch, just will the changes to happen. Do they? The mirror task involves finding a mirror and looking in it. What do you see? Move and watch what happens to your reflection. Walk through the mirror and see what's on the other side. In the television task, you find a television and experiment with it, adjust the sound, picture, color, and so on.

The main reason to do these tasks, aside from having fun, is to learn to act consciously in your dreams and, if you want, begin to control them.

Directing a Dream

One of the techniques for directing dreams is the same as one used for staying in a dream—spinning. If you want to visit someone, such as an ancient Tibetan master or Jesus in Galilee or Albert Einstein, you can spin in your dream with the intention of going there. You will often find yourself where you want to be.

Directing a dream may just involve conscious interaction. For example, if you are being chased, you can stop running, turn around, and confront your pursuer. Ask who he is and why he's chasing you. If you're being attacked, you can decide to defend yourself, confront your attacker, or just surround him with love and compassion until he changes his behavior.

You can have fun with other dream themes like examination dreams or dreams of being naked in public. Changing your dream scenario may actually shift the corresponding situation in your everyday life.

Changing a Nightmare

The dreams many people want to control most are nightmares, particularly recurring ones. One technique involves giving the nightmare a resolution or making it end well. Of course, the potential problem with this technique is that the issue in your life creating the nightmare may just be avoided.

In one dream a man asked the tiger that was chasing him who it was. The tiger responded that it was his father, who didn't like the way he was living. By engaging with the tiger in the dream, the man was able to see both that he did not need to be pursued by his father's judgments, and that the tiger had some good points—there really were ways he could do things better. If instead of confronting the tiger this man had simply turned it into a kitten, he would have resolved the fear of the tiger in the dream but wouldn't have resolved the issue with his father's judgments in his waking life.

The mystics remind us of the truth of those immortal words of Franklin Roosevelt "The only thing we have to fear is fear itself." The Sufi mystic Jalaludin Rumi put it this way: "There is no cause for fear. It is imagination blocking you as a wooden bolt holds the

door. Burn that bar." Tibetan Buddhists often use dream work to confront fear, not to confront the image of the dream, and to realize that fear itself is the illusion.

If you use this technique when you are confronted with danger in a dream and feel afraid, don't worry about the characters in your dream. Simply remind yourself that the danger and your fear are illusions. This is similar to the bardo practice in the *Tibetan Book of the Dead*, in which the practitioner remembers that every-thing seen in the bardo state between life and death is illusion and, truly, the only thing you have to fear is fear itself. If you just confront the images in your dreams, new frightening images will appear. If you confront your fear instead, the experience of fear itself will disappear.

The Senoi people of Malaysia have a similar tech-nique. If you are dreaming of falling, they suggest you relax and enjoy the fall. Imagine that you will land gently in an interesting place. Change the dream from fear to excitement about a new adventure.

Knowing When You Awake

The experience of false awakening is very common for lucid dreamers. These dreamers know that they were dreaming but believe they have now awakened. The dreamer is quite convinced that he or she is awake, getting up to have a shower, prepare breakfast, and leave for the office. The majority of long-term lucid dreamers experience series of such "awakenings," almost as if they were in nesting dream dolls. Each awakening seems like it is the true one until the dreamer notices some small detail is out of place.

Lucid dreaming veterans learn to test reality in two ways: pain and gravity. If you can do something normally impossible, it is 99 percent certain that you are dreaming. If you hurt yourself, you are likely to be awake, so pinching yourself still seems to be one of the best tests. But even when the dreamer finally wakes up, there may be a surprise in store, in the form of a waking vision, which appears in the physical reality. Such visions, known as hypnopompic hallucinations, are not as uncommon as we might suppose, and they tend to occur when the brain cannot manage the content of a dream.

Lucid dreaming can bring you insight and adventure. See which of these techniques or combination of techniques works for you. As always, don't hesitate to create your own method for lucid dreaming.

DREAMS I WISH TO HAVE?
HAVE I HAD THEM?
ARE THEY WAITING FOR ME TO DREAM THEM?

Approaches to Lucid Dreaming

That God speaks to us through our dreams and our prayers is a theme that has lasted longer than the Christian belief. This understanding was originally conveyed in the Bible with the story of Jacob and the ladder. In this tale, Jacob dreamed of a ladder reaching up to heaven, with angels ascending and descending. This, of course, was a metaphor for the belief that dreams and prayers act as a bridge between the divine and the human, an idea that prevails in most religious belief systems. Sufis invoke the "spirit of guidance," who embodies the wisdom of all the illuminated souls. Thus, like winged messengers, our dreams take flight at night to the universal source of divine knowledge, returning with advice to help guide us through the confusions of everyday life. The concept of the Akashic records, which we talked about in Chapter 1, envisages a vast, indeed infinite "library" containing the thoughts, dreams, prayers, and events of all time

and all beings in the universe, and forms the basis for karma between lives and those beings.

The shamans of Paleolithic cultures would turn to their dreams to get guidance on the next day's hunt. Both the Greeks and the Egyptians made pilgrimages to sacred dream sanctuaries, where they sought visitation from a god in a dream to cure their illnesses through the practice of dream incubation. The ancient Egyptians worshiped Serapis, the god of dreams, and built temples to him. In Greece dream interpretation was considered one of the important signs of civilization, and dream incubation became a highly developed art. People traveled from around the world to the famous shrines dedicated to the god of healing, Aesculapius; they underwent elaborate purification ceremonies before sleeping in his temple.

The technique of dream incubation—before falling asleep formulating a question to be answered in one's dreams—tells us that within our psyches resides a wise oracle, a spirit of guidance, to whom we can turn for help. Though today we may not have temples for this practice we can draw upon the wisdom of the past in crafting our own dream incubation rituals. By showing our unconscious the same respect we would give to a priest or a goddess, we create the conditions that allow our spirit guides to speak to us. Indeed, dreams are a kind of ongoing conversation with our own souls. For this reason, when we work with our dreams, a gradual evolution in our consciousness occurs. It's as if the wisdom of nature within each of us is cooperating through our dreams to help us find the healing solution to our life dilemmas.

Once, while visiting an ashram south of Bombay, I, Philip Dunn, sat before a spiritual teacher who had been working with visitors from the United States and Europe, most of whom had come for the same reason I was there—some form of search for the inner life. The master had instructed many individuals in meditation and prayer, and he asked if I knew what prayer was. I hesitated, trying to formulate an answer I supposed might impress him with my superior virtues. What was prayer? What was prayer for me? What could prayer be for others in my world, or any world for that matter? Nothing came. He waited for my response. Perhaps prayer was contemplation. Perhaps it was a silent awareness of truth. Perhaps it was a mystical essence that eluded me and had something to do with God or stillness. Somehow the words would not form into anything that could make any sense, let alone make him feel that I was a good subject for his wisdom.

So without further ado I told him I didn't know what prayer was, but I did know what it wasn't. I felt that when I was thinking I wasn't praying, and when I was worrying I wasn't praying. I felt that when I was rushing around as an achiever, I probably wasn't praying either. In fact, come to think of it, pretty much everything I did in my life wasn't praying!

He smiled benevolently, exactly the way one would expect such a being to smile. It seems that not knowing the true nature of prayer is the first step to learning and understanding what it is. Like Alcoholics Anonymous tells its students, the first thing you have to do to recover from alcoholism is admit that you drink too much. The first thing I had to do was to admit that I didn't know.

The teacher went on to tell me that, actually, all I needed to do to learn the true nature of prayer was realize that I was constantly in a state of prayer, whether I knew it or not, and all the thinking and feeling, doubting and worrying was prayer that was begging the divine existence around me to help me relax: "Please, God, help me to stop worrying, chattering in my mind; and give me some relief from these constant habits that prevent me from enjoying my life!"

It became clear to me over the following years that everything actually *is* prayer of one sort or another, and that as we become more and more aware of this, we open up the gaps between the thoughts, fears, and doubts—gaps where silence exists—and allow a kind of divine intervention that provides us with more opportunities to be still.

Humanity has, since the beginning of time, yearned for peace, for some sort of break from the moment-to-moment round of activities and troubles we envisage that our lives are made from. "God, if only I could take a break!" "My God, I have so much to do, it's obvious that I'll never get a vacation!" "When will I find some little bit of peace in all of this?" Most of us have uttered such prayers regularly, though we have not seen them as prayers. We are taught that prayer must take place in some rarefied environment or condition, and in some religions it is even said that an individual cannot speak directly to God but must do so only through a priest. The truth is that we speak to God constantly, for even the silences are a conversation with God.

Prayer is our language of the soul. It is our way of life, and although we may not think of it that way any longer because of changes in our belief system, it is probably the one remaining certainty of all religion. God, of course, in this context, is not a distant monolith of power but existence itself, within and outside our selves.

Several techniques for working with lucid dreams are efforts to control the dream state from the conscious mind. When we use prayer in dream work, we start from a different assumption: the realization that there is something greater than our conscious and individual minds, and that something—whether we call it Existence, God, Allah, Kuan Yin, or Jehovah—can help us, guide us, and tell us things we need to know, things we might not even think to ask. If you want to do dream work with this understanding, then you can pray for dreams, consciously or just with a yearning of your soul. The important thing is that you recognize that the dream state is a place where angels, literal or metaphorical, can bring you messages from a divine or greater source.

To pray consciously for a dream you can use the same basic techniques as other dream incubation methods. The difference is in your intention. Before you go to sleep, ask your question. It can be a specific question about something in your life, like "Should I take the new job?" "Should I marry Steve?" It can be a more philosophical or existential question, like "Can you help me understand the meaning of love more deeply?" or "What can I do to let go of past hurts that I'm holding on to?" Or you can make a request, such as "Can my daughter please be healed of cancer?" Any question or request that you find in your heart is appropriate to ask. The wording can also be your own. This is your heart speaking; words don't make much difference. In fact, you don't have to use words at all.

Hold the question or request in your mind and imagine yourself asking it to whatever image you have of the divine. We ask questions of God, Spirit, Existence, our higher self, or whatever we want to call this source of information and inspiration. We'll call it Spirit. Feel the energy of this Spirit and continue to ask or request as you fall asleep.

Asking Basic Questions

There are no right or wrong questions, but an important part of dream work is to ask the question

that will lead to the information you really want. When we ask Spirit a question, Spirit will give us a true and honest answer. But that answer will be useful to us only if we ask a real question.

For example, someone might ask, "How can I get the job at the insurance company?" If the true and honest answer is that she isn't supposed to work at the insurance company, she's supposed to sell her artwork, then the response to her question probably won't be very satisfactory to her. Chances are she won't dream about the job at all, or the dream won't be helpful in fulfilling her desire. She will then be tempted to say, "This doesn't work. I ask, but I don't get any help."

If a man asks the question "How can I get Susan to marry me?" and the truth is that he should marry Julia instead, he will most likely be disappointed by his dream work. If a woman asks how to work out the problems in her relationship, and the answer is that she's supposed to leave the relationship and be alone for a while, she's going to be likewise disappointed.

It's important to remember in any case that no answer at all may be a valuable answer: that we are asking the wrong questions for this point in our lives. We often believe we know what we want. We've made decisions, gotten training, found jobs, entered relationships or marriages. We have invested emotion, time, money, and effort in the decisions we have made, and because of these investments we aren't always open to hearing that our original decisions were wrong or flawed in some way.

Caroline Myss, the medical intuitive and teacher, talks about how she wanted to be a book publisher. She didn't even know there was such a thing as a medical intuitive, and the idea seemed pretty bizarre when she did hear about it. She had invested time and money in trying to become a publisher, and she didn't have money to live on while she established herself in some other kind of work. In spite of all these "impossibilities," she got strong messages to change her work. She listened to these messages, agreed to be a medical intuitive, and her new work expanded dramatically. She didn't have to set herself up, because as soon as she agreed to do this work, people started coming to her. If she hadn't listened to those messages, she would probably have gone through her life as a barely successful publisher, if she managed to succeed at all. Instead, she flowered into unknown talents and became an internationally known teacher.

Not everyone is destined for international fame, but everyone has a way of life that will make her or him happy and allow the greatest contribution in life. Spirit knows what that way of life is and will tell us, if we are willing to listen to the guidance. The first step in being willing is to take questions back to the most basic level. If you wonder about your work, try starting with a question like "What work will suit me best?" If your question is about a relationship or intimacy, ask, "Am I supposed to be in a relationship right now?" If the answer you get is yes, move on to a question like "Who will suit me best as a partner?" Try this as an experiment. You may be told that your current relationship is the right one for you at this time, but in asking, you make yourself available to whatever is right for you. That surrender, even in just asking the question, opens you to more and more information from Spirit.

For the purposes of dream work, it's often most effective to forget everything we think we know about our lives and turn ourselves over to Spirit. The only risk is that we will receive messages so clear and so clearly correct that we won't be able to avoid changing our lives! That isn't much of a risk, though, because when we are overwhelmed in this way, things tend to happen without much effort. Difficulty arises from trying to cling to the past, or trying to hold on to a way of doing things that no longer serves us.

Dream work is most effective when we have the courage to hear the truth, because Spirit speaks only the truth. Many of us are afraid of change, but courage is the willingness to go forward in spite of fear, not the absence of fear. If we have the courage to ask real questions and the courage to hear the true and honest answers, our lives will be transformed.

Finding a Question

Lie down in a comfortable position. Relax and breathe. Clear your mind and stop focusing on any problems or issues. See your thoughts as clouds in a clear blue sky on a windy day. The thoughts float into view and pass by. There is no need to engage with them. Just let them pass by in the blue sky. Keep breathing and relaxing. When your thoughts have become fewer and there are patches of blue in your inner sky, allow your question simply to arise on its own. Open yourself to Spirit and ask that the best question arise, then relax and let it emerge.

Once you know what your question is, write it down. Write it down exactly the way it came up. To impress the question on both your conscious and unconscious minds, you might want to put copies in places where you will see it throughout the day: on the refrigerator, the bathroom mirror, your computer. Write the question down again before you go to sleep, and put the piece of paper under the pillow. This reminds you that you want to seek the answer while you are asleep. Keep the question in your conscious thoughts as much as possible as you fall asleep.

After your question has come up, while you are still in a relaxed state, you might also want to suggest when you will remember the question in your waking state. For example, you could tell yourself that you will remember this question every time you open a door, because you are opening a door to a new part of your life. You might suggest that you will remember it every time you look at a clock or watch, because it is time to know the answer. (The unconscious mind seems to like the kind of wordplay that our conscious minds might find corny.) You can also choose a symbol to remind you of the question, then keep a picture of that symbol nearby while you're awake.

Remember that, as valuable as our dreamtime is, all our answers don't come when we are asleep. We often get answers in our waking state as well. Don't focus so much on dream work that you miss an answer that comes in another form. While you're paying attention to your dream work, remember to notice too the people you meet, things you are drawn to read, patterns that keep occurring, and sudden realizations. These may answer your question or help you understand your dreams.

Release Dreams and Message Dreams

There are two basic kinds of dreams: dreams that release stresses of the day or resolve unresolved conflicts, and dreams that bring a message or involve advanced dream work. A dream can serve both functions, of course, but in order to use advanced techniques of lucid dreaming or to use sleep time for meditative practices, the dreamer must move beyond dreams of release. This is because dream techniques require a certain consciousness that isn't possible in a release dream. A release dream is like a boiling kettle: Steam is given off because the pressure has built up to such an extent that it can no longer be held back. It pushes out with an uncontrolled force, and in dreams emotional issues and charges are let go.

For this reason, release dreams aren't very effective in giving answers to questions. If someone is asking about the right work to do without resolving issues about the stresses of his current work, his dreams about work might not give him the information he is seeking. If he mistakes a dream about resolving the stress of his current work for a dream about what he should do in the future, he might create difficulties for himself. It's essential to distinguish between dreams that are releasing tension and solving problems, and dreams that are answering questions.

No one can have consistently lucid dreams or get consistently reliable information from dreams while he or she is like a kettle on the boil. This is not to say that release dreams are bad. They give us a great deal of important information. We will be discussing ways you can work with release dreams and understand their messages in Chapters 7 and 8. In fact, most Western dream work has been with release dreams, examining what they reveal about our unconscious minds or the parts of our lives we aren't attending to enough. This is healing work, but it isn't the pinnacle of dream work.

In Chapter 2 we discussed some techniques for releasing stress before you sleep. A relaxed attention to release dreams and to the stresses or conflicts they are pointing toward is the best way to relieve emotional pressure and allow yourself the space to use your dreams for more advanced work. This is the same way that we deal with our waking lives. If you meet a friend who is crying about an upsetting situation, you don't talk about the party you're giving next week. When someone is very upset, she has to deal with or talk about the situation that is upsetting her before she will be calm enough to talk about more ordinary things. In a similar way, when we haven't dealt with something in the waking state or haven't wanted to admit to being upset, the disturbance will force its way to the surface when we sleep. If we honor that process, listen to it, and use it—just as we honor our friend and allow her to talk about what's upsetting her—our emotions will calm down and Spirit will be able to speak to us.

We can use conscious dream work techniques with release dreams as well as with lucid dreams. While there is a strong emotional pressure, it won't be easy to direct dreams, but it is possible to use consciousness to help reduce the pressure. If you can stay centered in your dream, a little distant from its story, you can allow issues to arise and play out, without being swept away by them. When you play the role of the witness in your dreams, issues are resolved more quickly.

Once the first level of stress has been released, secondary causes of stress arise. If you stay centered and watching, they will resolve and pass by as well. After a while you will find you have more clarity in your dreams and more space to seek new information. This is the point when dream incubation and lucid dreaming becomes possible.

Efforts to Control Dreams

Some people approach work with dream incubation as if the goal is for the conscious mind to control the experiences in the dream state. There are good reasons not to think of it quite that way. If we understand that our conscious minds are just a small part of our real consciousness or, to put it another way, that Spirit knows a lot more than we do, then we have a respect for what lies beyond our conscious minds.

Dreams are one realm in which we can connect with this wisdom. If we try to become conscious in our dreams for the purpose of controlling everything from the perspective of the conscious mind, then we lose the opportunity to learn. The motivation to control dreams in this way is a fear of the truth that is waiting for us beyond the world we already know.

People who have tried to control everything that happens in their dreams have sometimes been surprised to find that they can't do it. In one amusing story, a man realized that he was dreaming and thought that meant that he could do anything he wanted in the dream. He decided that he wanted to have sex and went looking for some women. He met two attractive women and told them he wanted to have sex with them, expecting them to agree readily. To his shock, they told him no. In spite of his surprise, he patiently explained that this was his dream and he could do what he wanted. They told him that was ridiculous. He ended up apologizing to them for his rudeness.

This dream has several implications. One is that we may not be able to control dreams in the way we think. Another is that the people we meet in the dream state may not be merely figments of our imagination. They may be other people who are also in the dream state, entities in another realm, or perhaps images controlled by a will that is greater than ours. The dreamer who

wanted sex was looking for pleasure without much, if any, regard for the women in his dream, whom he thought of as impersonal fantasies. He was refused, and this rebuff was a message beyond what he could have gained if the dream really could have been controlled by his conscious mind.

The conscious mind plays a role in conscious or lucid dreaming. The decision to do dream work, to ask questions, or to use dreamtime for meditative practices is a conscious decision. The conscious mind helps facilitate this process but does not really control it. For example, if a dreamer decides to ask to visit the Akashic records, the request is a conscious one, and the dreamer may use a technique to facilitate the journey, but if the dreamer tries to control what he finds when he gets to the records, the whole purpose will be defeated. The conscious mind only initiates and requests; after that, it surrenders to Spirit and allows information to come that is beyond its ability to achieve.

Whether you are on a dream quest or want to expand your spiritual practice, lucid dreaming techniques can bring rewarding results. Take your time with these techniques and be patient. The results will be worth it.

f i v e

Lucid Dreaming Adventures

After you have mastered the many techniques of lucid dreaming—you become aware of when you are dreaming and can stay in the lucid dream and direct it—then you're ready for more advanced adventures in the dream state.

FINDING INFORMATION

We have discussed the remarkable sources of information some people can access in their dreams. Now we will examine specific techniques for finding information in your dreams.

Questions

We talked in Chapter 4 about one of the most common uses of lucid dreaming: to get answers to questions or find information you want. You can do this by holding your current question in your mind as you fall asleep, but if you find yourself in a lucid dream, you can also direct the dream to answer the question. The techniques for doing this are limited only by your imagination. You can just ask the question and wait for the answer to come. You can spin in the dream while asking the question, with the intention of moving to the place where your question will be answered. You can hold the question in your mind while you turn on a television or view a movie screen in your dream, or even while you surf an imaginary Dreamnet. All of these approaches are basically the same: you are consciously asking your question while waiting or visualizing some way for the answer to come to you. Any way of getting an answer that appeals to you will probably be effective.

Search

You can also set off in search of information in your dreams, with the idea that the search or the dream quest is part of the process. A classic example is a visit to the Akashic records. Edgar Cayce and many others have spoken about them, or some similar source, where all the information we could possibly want has been recorded. The story of the Sibylline Prophecies, which foretold human history for thousands of years, is another example. These sources, said to be available in the conscious dream state, can tell us about the past, the present, and the future. They can give us new technology or recover old ways of doing things.

To access this information we must travel to its location in a conscious dream state and seek what we want. In Cayce's time the information was available in books. To the modern dreamer, it may well be available on a searchable database. The keys to reaching the information seem to be an intention of finding it, an openness to receiving it, and the visualization of some method of accessing it.

If the information you are seeking involves a place—for example, you want to know the best area for you to live, the best place for you to work, or the right house to buy or rent—you can find it by traveling there in your dreams and looking around you. You can read signs or talk to people you meet to find out where you are. If you like the place in your dreams, you might want to visit it in the waking state and see if you feel the same way.

Teachers and Guides

Another way conscious dreamers have their questions answered and find information is by meeting people in their dreams who act as teachers and guides. These people can answer questions, take the dreamers to where they will find what they seek, or can give fairly long and complex teachings. Some conscious dreamers set off to meet with historical figures like Jesus, Buddha, or Socrates. Some dreamers meet the same teacher or guide on more than one occasion; others meet him or her only once. Sometimes the guide will give something symbolic, like a necklace or an object of power that can help the dreamers with whatever issues they have in their lives.

TAPPING CREATIVITY

Dreams also have a potential for creative work. We don't usually think of being creative in our dreams, but these techniques might surprise you.

Artistic Pursuits

There are many stories about writers and painters who got new ideas in the dream state, but dream creativity isn't just for professional artists. You can tap into creativity in any part of your life. Most of us have some area of creativity: cooking, sewing, home improvement, gardening, gift wrapping, or many other everyday activities. We can get creative ideas for anything we enjoy in the dream state.

One painter visits dream galleries, where she views the next new things in art and picks out the style that she is going to try next. She gets virtually all of her ideas from these dream journeys. Another artist tries out a variety of techniques in her dreams. She attempts a painting in acrylic or watercolor or in a variety of color schemes. She has already tried and eliminated many possibilities before she ever begins a project in the waking state.

These techniques can be used for any creative project. In a lucid dream you can paint your house in a variety of colors and see how you like it. You can plant your garden, then move it through the seasons. If its form in one season doesn't suit you, you can back up and modify the planting. You can visit dream gardens, then find out what plants are used and how they are cared for. If you want to make a quilt, you can view as many quilts as you want in any styles that you like until you find the one that will be your next project.

If you are a professional writer or artist or would like to be, your dream resources can be invaluable to you. If you've often dreamed of writing a book, but aren't sure what it should be about, you can go to the book in the dream state and read parts of it, or the topic or story can be presented or acted out for you in your dream. Whole poems and story lines have been transmitted in this way. Likewise, if you've always wanted to be a visual artist, at least in your leisure time, but you're not sure what form of art would really suit you, you can try out a variety of media in your dreams. You can paint, sculpt, or throw pots and see how you do.

The dream state may be particularly good for creativity because the critic and censor that is often so present in the waking state has less power in a dream. There is also no worry about how things will turn out because they aren't "real." You don't have to buy the paints or take a ceramics class to try out painting or pottery in your dreams, and you don't have to dispose of failed projects. No one else can see what you're doing unless you let someone into your dreams, so you feel more free to try new things and to make mistakes.

LUCID DREAMING ADVENTURES

Problem Solving

Another use for the conscious dream state is problem solving. Most of us have heard stories of scientists who have made great discoveries in their dreams, but this space is just as useful for those of us who will never be nominated for a Nobel Prize. One medical student used the dream state to sort out many of the math and science problems from his classes during the first two years of medical school. He finished his work with surprising accuracy and got more sleep than his fellow students.

They might not be scientific or mathematical problems, but we all have things to work out. How can you juggle your time to take that art class and still get your work done and the kids to their activities? What would be the best way to remodel the kitchen? Which car is the best buy? Why is your computer malfunctioning? You could pose the last as a question and go see a dream computer expert, but if you have sufficient information, your mind may just solve the problem for you while you sleep.

Without the distractions of the waking state, where we can rarely concentrate on one idea for long without some interruption, our minds can sort through all the information we have when we are conscious. They can also connect with other sources of information and bring us new, creative solutions to our problems.

PRACTICING PHYSICAL AND PROFESSIONAL SKILLS

While you're dreaming, you may be lying there completely relaxed, but you can still practice physical and professional skills.

Sports and Motor Skills

Major athletes, like Olympic contenders and professionals, discovered dream practice long ago. They can use it to sort out problems, try new techniques, and perfect old ones. This dream activity is as beneficial for amateur athletes and couch potatoes as it is for the professionals.

Do you want to learn to skate or ski without falling down a lot? Are you tempted to try out one of those super skateboards or scooters but don't want to make a fool of yourself? You can practice and perfect those motor skills before you ever expose your backside to concrete or your ego to the derision of your friends. You can do this both by visualizing the activity while in a relaxed waking state and by consciously selecting an activity while you're in a lucid dream. If you want to dream of learning a motor skill, try thinking about it and visualizing yourself in your chosen activity while you fall asleep. You can give yourself the suggestion that as soon as you're doing the activity without effort you'll know you're asleep and will become lucid in the dream. Once you become lucid, you can select the skills you want to practice more easily.

Probably the best thing about this kind of dream activity is that it has a real effect on the body. That makes it a great alternative for couch potatoes and those who can never find the time to exercise. Try running for exercise and pleasure in your dreams. You can imagine any setting you want: fields of wildflowers, forests with bubbling streams, or extraterrestrial landscapes. You can be joined by deer, a wolf, a Martian, or your best friend, spouse, or lover. Run with the expectation and intention of waking up energized and rested. You might be surprised to find that you want to get more exercise in the waking state after enjoying it so much in the dream state.

Many of us have negative associations with exercise because we weren't successful in sports, didn't enjoy physical education classes, or have tried to do what didn't suit us. It's all too common for people to decide to diet and exercise just before summer and to end up sore, exhausted, or injured. We can release many of these bad associations by creating new experiences in the dream state. We find that not only can we hit the ball when playing tennis but we can slam it, and we have a killer serve. We can run as fast and as far as we want without one stitch in the side, and we can climb Everest without a rope or the danger of frostbite. In short, in dreams we can enjoy the strength of our bodies without physical limitations. The pleasure of these experiences can lead us to enjoy the movement of our bodies more in the waking state.

Professional and Everyday Skills

We can also practice other kinds of physical skills, experiment, modify, and practice some more in our dreams. This ability is particularly wonderful for those of us who find there aren't enough hours in the day to do all the things we need and want to do. By practicing skills in the dream state, we can become more efficient. One surgeon who uses this technique finds himself highly sought after because he performs operations faster than his colleagues, lowering the risk to patients by having them in surgery for a shorter time. By the time he gets to the operating room, he has tried several possibilities and knows the fastest and best way to perform the operation.

If you are sometimes scattered or disorganized, dream practice can help you get organized. If you're already organized, dream practice will help you perfect your skills. You can also save time and effort by attempting new things in your dreams. For instance, you can try out new recipes in your dream kitchen, and adjust and improve them before you ever try them in the waking state.

Could you get more done at work if you could type faster or use a calculator more efficiently? Are you learning to drive an SUV after years of driving a compact car and need to polish your skills? Do you need to improve your baseball pitching or volleyball skills before the next office summer party? Whatever it is you'd like to improve, you can practice and perfect your skills in the dream state.

HEALING

Healing is one of the areas that concern all of us at some time in our lives. If we aren't in need of healing ourselves, we have loved ones who are. Throughout history and many cultures, people have used the dream state as a place to heal and to find remedies. We can do the same. These techniques can turn your dreamtime into a time of healing:

Visualization

Visualization involves seeing ourselves or others as healed, healing, recovered, or as if we or they have never suffered an accident or illness. A dancer once injured her foot by landing wrong in practice. The doctors told her that she would have to be off the foot for several months. Since she couldn't afford to be out of work for so long, she visualized doing the move where she was injured over again, but doing it correctly. She did this visualization in both a waking state and in the dream state. Because she repeatedly gave her foot the message that it was never injured, it healed quickly and she was back at work in weeks.

With cancer, visualization is often used in conjunction with other healing techniques. Some people have been very successful in visualizing their own tumor or someone else's shrinking, dissolving, and disappearing. Visualization has also been used in cases of severe back injury where there was a question of whether the person would ever walk again, as well as for more minor injuries.

To use this technique in the dream state, it is often helpful to begin the visualization before falling asleep and to move from the waking to the dreaming state while holding the image. In the dream state, when we become conscious and lucid we can see and experience the body as whole, healed, and vibrant.

It is good to consider all the possible outcomes from a visualization so you don't produce a result you don't want. One physician in California discovered that he was a hands-on healer, and because of his scientific background, he wanted to study and understand the healing process. He set up an experiment in which he worked with cultures of infection-causing bacteria and viruses. He thought that if he infused the cultures with loving-kindness, he would stop the infection. He found that, to the contrary, the bacteria and viruses flourished. The infections became worse if the bacteria and viruses were given support. He had to be very clear

what result he intended when he transmitted energy to the ill or injured body. In the same way, you need to be very clear about the result you are visualizing.

Communicaton with the Body

In our busy lives we often get out of touch with our bodies. We don't give them the nutrients, the exercise, or the attention they need. This neglect can often result in illness or injury. To heal the body it is sometimes necessary to get back in touch with it, ask it what it needs, and begin to relate to it in a different way. It's always good to start with an apology for all the times we haven't paid attention to the body and to take the time to really appreciate it. If we just lie still and tune in to the body, we begin to be aware of all the amazing things it is doing while we are distracted. The lungs are bringing in oxygen and taking out waste, the blood is transporting the oxygen to the cells, fighting off intruders, and carrying waste out of the cells. The rest of the immune system is working with the blood, while various organs convert our food to usable energy, produce hormones and other chemicals, remove waste and toxins, and keep us going. Most of the time we don't pay attention to any of this and just get irritated when the body doesn't do what we want. We might eat junk food, and then resent the body when our energy levels drop. We are not consciously aware of how this kind of food affects our bodies or what our bodies have to do to compensate for a poor diet. Our thoughts, particularly our stresses and tensions, also affect the body, but we aren't very aware of that effect either.

Once we tune in to what our body is doing for us, appreciate it, and realize that we haven't been paying enough attention, we are ready to talk with the body and find out what we need to do differently to heal. It's important to remember that this practice is about listening, not dictating. At least one person got even more ill while using this process, because she was trying to tell the body how she wanted it to heal. At the beginning she was just a little bit ill. When she attempted to dictate to her body, she found herself unable to get out of bed. Once she realized her mistake and asked her body to make the decisions, she recovered fully. The point is that illness has arisen because the body is not being listened to, and it's essential not to make the situation worse.

If you are really appreciative of your body and really receptive to what it has to say, you can get invalu-

able information about health and healing from your body, and it will be information uniquely suited to your body, body type, and situation. We've all heard contradictory opinions on matters of health; what better authority to sort it all out than your own body?

To do this process, tune in to your body, notice what it is doing for you, allow yourself to feel appreciation, and begin to ask your body what it would like you to do. It may give you this information while you are still awake, or you can fall into sleep while asking the question. If you find yourself in a lucid dream, you can do the same process in the dream state and hear the body's messages there.

A Journey Inside

Another way of learning about your body, either to find out what's wrong or to deepen your appreciation of it, is to take a journey inside. You can travel in a boat down your bloodstream, float into your lungs, climb up and down your spine, or do anything else you can imagine. Traveling inside the body is such an appealing idea that movies have been made about it.

Your body is a fascinating and complex organism that will provide you with new frontiers to explore for a very long time. If you aren't interested in that kind of knowledge, you can simply use the technique to tune in to where the difficulty is and explore it.

Healers and Expert Information

Like teachers and guides, healers are available in the dream state. They can actually heal you in the dream or can give you techniques or information you need to heal. You can travel to where the healers are or ask them to come to you in the dream state. If you are on a dream journey to find how to heal, you might meet a healer without intending to.

Healers may be humans, spirits, or animals, and their form may have to do with your expectations. If you are a Christian who expects help to come in angelic form, your healer might well be an angel. If you are interested in shamanic healing, the healer might come as your power animal or an animal or spirit that is important to you. If you are a Buddhist, Gautama, Kuan Yin, or Tara might come to help you.

Healing information, like all other information, can be obtained from both healers and other dream sources. Edgar Cayce used the Akashic records mostly to get information to help other people heal. He would

find information about their lives, their bodies, and the exact treatment they needed located in the records he consulted.

SPIRITUAL AND MEDITATIVE PRACTICES

Many traditions, as we have seen, use the sleep state for spiritual and meditative practices. Here are some techniques you can experiment with to use dreamtime for meditation and spiritual work.

Practicing Techniques

When you become lucid in a dream, you can choose to do whatever spiritual practice you prefer. You can pray, enter into Christian contemplation, do the Sufi dhikr practice, chant a mantra like om mani padma hum, repeat the names of Amida Buddha, or do some more complex practice. If you want to deepen your meditation or prayer, for example, you can experiment in your dreams with ways to do that or suggest that you will find yourself more centered and find your meditation deepening.

Some dreamers have visualized themselves going through their everyday lives but staying centered in a spiritual practice at the same time. It is more difficult to stay centered in waking life, but by doing so in the dream state, they were able to obtain a new perspective on their lives. The small things that normally irritate or distract were not nearly so troubling while the practitioner was centered in prayer or meditation. This experience can carry over to the waking state.

Following the Golden Thread

You can visualize and follow a golden thread that leads to your highest nature. This inner nature might be thought of as the seventh mansion of the soul that Teresa of Avila wrote about, the ultimate emptiness of Mahayana Buddhism, the Atman of Hinduism, or some more general concept of Being. However you think of it, this part of yourself can be reached, in part, through dream journeys in which you follow the trail or thread to your inner Truth.

When you become conscious in a dream and wish to begin such a journey, search for the golden thread or spin with the intention of moving to the place where you can find the thread. Begin to follow the thread and be aware of what arises for you. What are the obstacles? Who helps you along the way? This can be a healing and transformational journey.

Dream Work Techniques

The first step in doing good dream work is to get a good night's sleep, so that you are well rested. It's best not to drink stimulants like coffee, tea, or soft drinks containing caffeine late in the day and not to eat foods high in carbohydrates or sugar too late in the evening. It's best to make your last meal as light as possible, and some people find it relaxing to take a walk after dinner, particularly if they haven't had too much exercise during the day.

Try to make your bedroom as pleasant as possible—a place where you feel comfortable and relaxed. The room should be painted and decorated in colors that you find relaxing. Clean up clutter in the room and keep your sheets fresh. You might want to try aromatherapy, use a scented eye pillow, or keep a vase of flowers on the bedside table. The room should be well ventilated, not stuffy but not too cold. Take time to set up your sleeping area with care.

Some people think you should sleep with your head to the north so that you are aligned with the magnetic currents of the planet. You might want to see if doing so makes any difference to you. The bed should be comfortable for you, not too hard or soft. The really important thing is that you feel comfortable and relaxed and that your sleeping area is a place you want to go when you're tired.

It's best if your sleeping place really is for sleeping and is not a place you bring last-minute work from the office or watch late-night television. You will fall asleep more easily if you don't watch disturbing or controversial programs right before bedtime or do work that takes a lot of mental focus. A racing mind needs time to calm down before you can fall into a restful sleep. In the same way, frightening stories or thrillers don't make restful bedtime reading. Try to go to bed when you're tired and not wait until you're exhausted. For some people it's best to go to sleep on a schedule. For others it's better to go to bed when they feel tired. See what works best for you.

If you find that you are tense or your mind is racing when you want to go to sleep, try relaxation techniques like tensing parts of your body and then relaxing them, imagining each part of your body relaxing, imagining yourself walking down a stairway to a place of relaxation, or counting from one to ten or one to a hundred. There are countless techniques available for relaxation. You might also want to use music or a recording of a guided relaxation or meditation. Experiment and see what you like and what makes you sleep best and feel most rested in the morning.

Because we all forget many of the details of our dreams within minutes of waking, it's also important to have some means of recording your dream where you can reach it as soon as you wake up. The sooner you record your dreams, the more information you will have to interpret them, and you may record dreams you would otherwise forget altogether. You might want to use a notebook or a small, easy-to-operate tape recorder. A tape recorder is particularly useful if you wake in the night but don't want to turn on the light or focus your eyes enough to write in a notebook. The recording will allow you to write the details of your dreams in your notebook when you have more time.

Your dreams will often relate to what is happening in your life at the time, so it can also be helpful to keep a short journal. You can write a few paragraphs about

the most important aspects of each day and keep it in the notebook with your dreams. By keeping track of what's happening in your life in relation to your dreams, you may see patterns emerge. For example, you may find that a recurring chase dream always happens after you've had an argument with your husband or been involved in a particularly stressful situation at work.

DREAM MEMORIES

Dream work begins with remembering and recording your dreams. That sounds easy, but it can take some work in the beginning.

Remembering Your Dreams

Many people say, "I don't dream" or "I never remember my dreams." The truth is that we all dream and we all sometimes remember a dream, though we might not remember it for long. It's also true that we can all learn to remember our dreams long enough to record them. Understanding that we can remember dreams is often the first step to doing it. If we expect to remember our dreams, chances are we will. Because of that, it's often effective to repeat to yourself while you're falling asleep that you will be able to remember your dreams. The dream state is when your unconscious mind talks to your conscious mind, and the twilight zone between sleeping and waking is when the conscious mind has the best opportunity to talk to your unconscious mind. If you suggest to your unconscious mind that you will remember what you dream that night, it is very likely that you will remember.

When you decide to do dream work, it's a good idea to make a commitment to it for a reasonable length of time, say six months. Like pretty much everything else we do, dream work takes time to learn to do well. In six months you should be able to get a lot of benefit from your dream work, and the chances are good that you won't want to stop. Our greatest resistance to dream work comes at the beginning, when we may be consciously or unconsciously a little afraid of digging too deeply into our dreams.

If you find that you are resistant to remembering your dreams or that you sometimes feel lazy about recording them, make a commitment to yourself that you will record something whenever you wake up, whether you remember a dream or not. Record how you felt when you woke up, what you were thinking

about, and images you remember. This information can trigger a memory of a dream. Also, if your unconscious realizes that you are going to record something anyway, you will most likely find yourself remembering dreams.

Since we have somewhere from three to twelve dreams in a night, it isn't likely that you'll want to record every dream you have. If you find yourself remembering several dreams each morning, decide how much material you want to work with and record the dreams you think are most important or interesting. You can also tell your unconscious that you want to remember only one dream a week or one dream a night, or whatever works for you. Then your unconscious will be selecting the dream for your conscious mind to consider. If you'd rather have your conscious mind do the choosing, ask to remember all or many of your dreams, then select which ones you want to record and work with.

If possible, try to wake up without an alarm clock. An alarm rouses you before a dream can finish, but when you wake naturally, you've finished your dreams. When you're getting enough sleep, you should be able to wake up in the morning without artificial help. If you don't do it naturally, you can tell yourself what time you want to wake up as you are relaxing to go to sleep. You'll find that your body's internal clock is amazingly accurate. If you do need some help to wake up, try using something, like a CD alarm that plays very gentle, soothing music. Be sure to allow enough time in the morning to make at least a quick recording of your dreams.

Recording Your Dreams

You can record your dreams in as much detail as you have the time and energy to write down. The more details you have, the more information will be available for you to understand what the dream is trying to tell you. These details can include the plot, the images, the characters and what they looked like, the location, and very important—how you felt during all the parts of the dream. Who else was in your dream? What did they look like? What were they doing? What colors did you see? Some dream interpretation books have checklists to use in recording your dreams. It's best not to use anyone else's form unless it really suits you, but lists can give you ideas of what works best for you. Some people, for example, almost never dream in color, but when they do it's significant. They may always want to

ask themselves, "Was there any color?" You'll discover the kinds of details most useful for your interpretations.

If you decide to do a detailed interpretation of one dream a week, you could write that dream in a journal, along with notations about what happened to you that week. You could do something similar if you want to interpret one dream a day. There is no right way to do dream interpretation and no formula that works for everyone. The best thing you can do is to experiment and find the way you feel most comfortable.

DREAM WORK

There are several things to consider when you decide how you want to do your dream work. Do you want to work with a partner or a group? Should you rely on the "experts"?

Dream Partners

It can sometimes be very helpful to have someone to talk to about your dreams. Just telling someone else about your dream can be enough to trigger an understanding of what the dream means. When we have a dream, we experience it from the inside. When we tell the dream to someone else, we have to talk about it in an objective way. Just that change of perspective is often enough to give us major insights.

Talking to someone about your dreams, though, is very intimate. You are exposing your deepest fears and desires and your most embarrassing worries. You need to make sure that your dream partner is someone you can trust to keep your dreams in confidence. If you dream about sleeping with your best friend's husband, that might not be something you want your best friend or your husband to hear about. In fact, the dream might not indicate a real desire to sleep with your friend's husband. It might mean that you're feeling competitive with your friend, or that her husband has some trait you've been wishing that your own husband had. To discover the real meaning of your dreams you need a safe place to examine them. So choose a dream partner carefully.

Your dream partner should also be someone who wants to help you understand your own dreams and not interpret them for you. There is no set way of working with a partner, but it's good to keep in mind that we all have to decide for ourselves what our dreams mean. If your partner wants to tell you what your dream would mean to her or him, and you find

that meaning helpful in getting in touch with your own feelings about the dream, that's fine. Be careful, though, of anyone who wants to tell you what it means for you.

If you decide to work on one dream a week, you might want to set up a time with your dream partner when you talk about the dreams you are each looking at that week. You might also simply call each other when you're having difficulty understanding a dream or when you want to talk about a dream you're excited about. You might want to have several dream partners that you talk to about different kinds of dreams. Anything that works for you is fine.

Dream Groups

Dream groups, like dream partners, are worthwhile only if they are helpful to you. Choose a group where you feel completely comfortable, safe, and supported. If you feel too vulnerable or tense, the group process will probably be more of a hindrance than a help. Groups can be even more challenging to work with than partners. You have to be confident that everyone in the group will protect your privacy or you will find yourself revealing only your less embarrassing dreams and missing much of the benefit of the work. In a group you also have several people, instead of just one, who might impose their interpretations on your dream.

None of these obstacles is insurmountable, however, and many people find dream groups very helpful. Set up the group in a way that works best for all of you. If you like structure, set your group up with rules and guidelines. If you feel more comfortable with an informal discussion format, use that.

The only thing you really need to keep in mind is that each of us is the best judge of what our dreams mean. We may have a very clear idea of what someone else's dream means and be convinced that we're right. If so, we'll want to tell them what the dream means. In reality what we see in someone else's dream is usually our own projection of our symbols and metaphors. It's true that we sometimes have intuitive insights that are helpful to other people, but it's often hard to tell the difference between a projection and an insight. The dreamer knows what the dream means and will know when the meaning is revealed. So if insights are offered as considerations instead of as statements of truth, they can be helpful. All we need is the respect to let each person decide her truth for herself. If members of a

dream work group have that basic respect for one another, the chance are good that they will be able to do pretty amazing work together.

Dream Analysis

You will need to develop your own way of dream interpretation. If books are useful for you, then use them. If not, don't worry. There isn't a right way to do it. Some people work well with structure or with written material. Others work best without structure and with visual material. If you're the first kind of person, you might want to write as many details of your dreams into your journal, along with what's been happening in your life. Then you can go over the material, maybe outlining it or making lists of images, colors, characters, dialogue, plot, and so on.

Or you could lie back in a comfortable place and run the dream again in your head. You might stop the action, look more closely, ask different characters what they're feeling, or become another character in your dream. If this kind of replay works better for you than written descriptions, use it. If some combination of the two works better for you, use that. Trust yourself in finding the way that works best for you.

Since we all have our own systems of images and metaphors, it is often a good idea to keep track of the symbols in your dreams and begin to compile a personal dream dictionary. Don't assume, though, that your unconscious uses the same symbol the same way in every dream. You are always changing and growing, so stay flexible and open to the meanings of symbols and metaphors as they may evolve.

Other Resources

If you want to read dream books or dream dictionaries, consult interpreters, or research mythology or psychology, by all means do so. Whatever you feel drawn to will probably be helpful to you, even if it isn't helpful in the way you expect it to be. You might want to consult your dreams by asking what are the best ways for you to understand your dreams and the best resources to use.

The most important thing to remember is to relax and have fun. If you're enjoying your dream interpretation and feeling grateful for the information you're receiving, you are likely to get more and more useful information. So, tune in, associate, feel, and have a great time discovering your inner realms.

THE DREAMS OF MY HEART AND SOUL:
DREAMS I'VE HAD MORE THAN ONCE

s e v e n

Dream Theories

When you decide to interpret your dreams or to receive the information they are sending to you, the most important thing to remember is that they are your dreams. Some of your dreams will be obvious; you will know right away what they are about. Often you will have dreams that are at first incomprehensible. That's when you say to your family or friends, "I had the strangest dream last night." This is because your unconscious mind communicates differently than your conscious mind. It likes to use images, colors, symbols, and metaphors.

Remember that these are *your* images, colors, symbols, and metaphors, they are not from some universal dream book. Just as you have a personal way of speaking, writing, and relating to others, you have a personal way of dreaming. We cannot say it often enough: Ultimately, only you can decipher the meaning of your dreams.

Still, when it is difficult to decipher dreams, you may be tempted to use all the resources available from people who claim to be experts. You need to be careful to choose the real interpretation yourself. In order to evaluate the help people are offering you, you must know what theory of dreams they are using. If you don't agree with their theories keep that in mind when you evaluate their input.

THE THEORY OF SYMBOLS

Symbol theory says that not only does the unconscious mind dream in symbols but those symbols are universal. This perspective has resulted in many books, often called dream dictionaries, which give pat explanations for everything in dreams. Symbol theory is based on ancient interpretations of dreams that arose in small societies that often shared a basic culture and religion. Perhaps people in those times did share set symbols and mythology, but that is not true today.

In our global village, with huge libraries, the Internet, fast travel, and international communication, we are exposed to symbols and myths from many cultures and periods. It is very difficult to tell which myth or symbol is going to influence an individual at any point in time. Advocates of the symbol theory seem to argue that everyone's dreams are based on European history and myths. If you dream of a dragon, it will be interpreted according to European dragon lore, while your association may actually be with Chinese dragon myths.

Symbol theory is found in a variety of sources that you may or may not find useful.

Dream Dictionaries

Dream Dictionaries can be absurdly obvious. For example, one online dictionary says, "Suicide: When a dreamer dreams about suicide, then he probably does not want to live much longer." That's the literal meaning of suicide, but that is not necessarily what suicide means in a dream. A dream of suicide may be a message to you that you are not allowing a part of yourself to live, and in that sense you are committing a kind of suicide. By tuning in to the symbols, events, and plot of your dream, you can start to understand the metaphor you have created.

Biblical Symbolism

One area of symbol theory assumes that dreams can be interpreted based on the Bible. In our very pluralistic society, where people are often open to a wide variety of religious ideas, this is no longer very realistic. Even devout Christians often don't have sufficient familiarity with biblical texts to use detailed symbolism from them. For example, one biblical interpretation guide says that arrows in a dream are negative signs based on the books of Zechariah, Romans, Timothy, and so on. If you associate arrows with Robin Hood and his merry men overthrowing the forces of evil, arrows probably don't have a negative association for you, however they appear in the Bible. If when you think of some element in your dream you think of the Bible, then the Bible is a good place to look for symbols and associations. If you don't think of the Bible, there is no reason to assume that the metaphor your unconscious has created for you is to be found there.

The Meaning of Color

Another area of symbol theory is the belief that colors have specific meanings. For example, one dream dictionary says: "Gray indicates fear, fright, depression, ill health, ambivalence and confusion. You may feel emotionally distant or detached." No doubt gray does mean those things to some people, but it might not mean them to you. If your office, which you love, is decorated in soothing shades of pale gray, it may symbolize calm, peace, and quiet. If you wear gray a lot because you think it looks particularly good on you, it may symbolize being at your best or putting your best foot forward. Only you know what your association is with the color gray.

Some of the meanings given for colors can be amusing. For example, "The appearance of hot pink color in your dream represents sex and lust." As with all other aspects of dream interpretations, follow your own ideas and feelings about color.

PSYCHOLOGICAL THEORIES

Dream interpretation went out of style in Europe from the Enlightenment to the Victorian era of the late nineteenth century. Dreams were thought to be nonsense, not worth worrying about, except perhaps as indications not to eat rich foods in the evenings. All of that was changed by Sigmund Freud (1856–1939) and his contemporaries. Two of them were students of Freud who later broke with him; they were Carl Jung (1875–1961) and Alfred Adler (1870–1937). The last great name in dream theory was Frederick (Fritz) Perls (1893–1970), who developed Gestalt therapy. Most of modern psychological theory on dreams is based on the theories of some or all of these psychologists. Some of their suggestions and insights can be useful, and it's also helpful to know the theories that underlie their approaches.

Sigmund Freud

Freud changed the understanding of dreams forever in his landmark work *The Interpretation of Dreams* (1900). He believed that dreams arise only in the unconscious, and they arise during sleep because our usual conscious defenses are down. For Freud the unconscious was a storehouse of repressed desires and urges that were able to come out only when our repressive vigilance was missing. Freud worked in the extremely sexually repressed culture of Victorian Vienna. So, not surprisingly, he believed that most of what people repress into the unconscious is about sex. That may actually have been the case with him and

134

many of his patients. For Freud any slender or elongated object in a dream, such as a stick, a knife, a cane, represented a phallus. Any cavity or receptacle, like a bowl, a cave, a cup, or even a room, represented a vagina. Any round objects, especially in pairs, like apples, balls, or pears, represented breasts.

Freud believed that dreams are about wish fulfillment. They might relate to desires to finish incomplete personality development, power struggles, love, or thoughts repressed during the day. Anxiety in dreams was usually interpreted as sexual anxiety. To determine what dreams were about, in addition to his imposed sexual symbolism, Freud used the revolutionary technique of free association, in which the patient would state anything that came to mind in relation to the dream object no matter how absurd it seemed or how embarrassing it was. Most modern Freudian therapists have toned down Freud's sexual imagery and use a modified form of dream interpretation.

Alfred Adler

Alfred Adler, like Sigmund Freud, was a Viennese physician interested in human psychology. He worked with Freud until 1911 but parted company with him

then because he didn't agree that sexuality is as important in human behavior as Freud insisted. For Adler, people were very goal oriented, with an urge toward personal growth and wholeness. Dreams, therefore, weren't just a way to work out repressions but part of the movement toward growth. He also saw that each individual developed a unique style for dealing with psychological issues. For him, determining this style was very important, and dreams were one way to do that. He called this approach Individual Psychology.

In Adler's theory, people often use dreams to work out conflicts between what they want and what is socially acceptable. So if they felt powerless, they might be aggressive in their dreams, even though that aggression wouldn't be acceptable in the waking state. To help determine the patient's individual style of dealing with things, Adler would look at whether the patient was active or passive, independent or dependent, or optimistic or pessimistic in the dream state.

Carl Jung

Carl Jung also studied under Sigmund Freud, but disagreed with him about the nature of the unconscious mind. For Freud it was instinctual and animalistic, a reservoir of repressed and distorted ideas. Jung, by contrast, believed that the unconscious is divided into two parts, the individual unconscious, a reservoir of repressed energy, and the collective unconscious, a reservoir of collective information that includes symbol and image, as well as information for spiritual transformation.

Jung also disagreed with Adler that the unconscious mind is trying to hide things from the conscious. Rather, he saw dreams as guides to waking life in our effort to achieve wholeness. They help with problem solving and give us information about ourselves.

Jung had a specific psychological theory that influenced his interpretations of dreams. He saw the self as divided into several parts, such as the persona, or image we present to the world; the shadow, the rejected aspects of the self; the anima, the repressed feminine aspects in the male psyche; the animus, the repressed masculine aspects in the female psyche; the divine child, the true self; the wise old man, the self or some other powerful figure; and the great mother, a symbol of growth, nurturance, fertility, seduction, or dominance. For Jung and his students, these aspects play an important part in dreams.

Jung also believed in archetypes, which he thought were images located in the collective unconscious that occurred in every culture and had a universal meaning. Images of the archetypes would include the mother, the god, the hero, and concepts of rebirth and renewal. These general meanings are very different from the specific meanings for images given in books and some interpretations. Archetypes are images that relate to the universal human experiences of birth, life, and death. For Jung, dream interpretation required a study of mythology, religion, and alchemy as well as of his psychological theories.

Frederick Perls

Frederick, usually known as Fritz Perls, the founder of Gestalt therapy, was another pioneer in understanding dreams. He was a German physician who studied Freudian psychoanalysis in Berlin before he broke away from Freud and criticized him in the book *Ego, Hunger and Aggression*. Perls advocated a natural, holistic approach to understanding the body and mind. He saw dreams primarily as a way of dealing with unfinished emotional business or what he called emotional holes. He thought the images in people's dreams were more influenced by their personal experiences than by the collective unconscious.

Perls escaped from Nazi Germany in 1933 and went to South Africa for the duration of World War II. After the war he immigrated to New York, where he met the psychologist Paul Goodman. Together they founded the Gestalt Institute in New York.

Gestalt Therapy had a very specific method for dream interpretation. The dreamer would imagine that the dream is a play on a stage and then would tune in to each part of the dream, animate or inanimate, to feel and speak for that part. For example, if someone dreamed she was a small girl building a sand castle and the ocean kept coming in and destroying her work, she might first say, "I'm a very small girl, and I feel very angry that you're so big and you keep ruining my castle." Then she might say, "I'm a sand castle and I feel very insecure. I could be washed away at any moment." Finally, "I'm the sea and I hate you. That's why I keep destroying your castle." Perls would even have the patient engage in dialogues between the parts of the dream. "I hate you." "I hate you, too, you're such a big bully." That would go on until the dreamer became aware of who the characters in the dream actually were.

For example, this dreamer might realize that the sea is her sister, the one who always bullied her and tried to control her.

Some Gestalt therapists now use group processes, in which people play the different parts in a dream. Some have also interpreted Perls's theory as meaning that all parts of a dream represent parts of the dreamer, possibly parts that have been disowned. For example, in the dream of the girl and her sand castle, the sea would have represented some part of the dreamer herself. It has to be her internal bully that she has disowned and not her sister. This simplistic theory is very limiting, considering that Perls's process was designed to allow the dreamer to discover for him or herself what the dream means.

Modern hypnotherapists, such as Milton Erickson and his students, believe that the unconscious mind uses metaphors and symbols in all its communications, not just to hide things from the conscious mind. Erickson found that hypnotic suggestions given in metaphors and symbols were much more powerful and long lasting than those given in a logical way. He would sometimes give suggestions in such an indirect manner that the patient didn't know anything had happened.

There is one story about how Erickson spent an entire session talking about the interconnectedness of the pattern on his tie. The patient was furious that he didn't get any help and refused to pay for the session. To his surprise, the problem with family relations—or interconnectedness and family ties—he had consulted Erickson about was resolved "spontaneously" over the next few months.

Each of these giants of psychological dream theory had important contributions to make to understanding dreams. This summary should give you the basic information you need to understand and evaluate the psychological theories that underlie books you may read or people you may work with in interpreting your dreams.

MY PSYCHOLOGIST DREAMS:
DREAMS I WOULD TELL MY SHRINK -
(IF I HAD ONE)

eight

Dream Interpretation

APPROACHES TO INTERPRETATION

Release dreams, as we said before, are those dreams that come to you spontaneously and often seem crazy and disjointed. These dreams have a lot of information for you, if you can decode them. Many different approaches to dream interpretation have been developed to do this decoding. To find the way that works best for you, try out a variety of these techniques.

Associations

You can try a Freudian-style free association to see what connections you have with things in your dreams. If you are being chased by Mafiosi, what ideas come to mind for you concerning the Mafia? Do you think of violence, anger, abuse of power? Or do you find the Mafia a bit romantic after having watched movies like *The Godfather*? As you examine your associations with the Mafia, you'll get a better idea of what you're

running from. If you associate the Mafia with anger, are you having issues with someone who can't control his or her anger? Do you feel vulnerable to danger in some area of your life? If you think the Mafia is a little exciting but dangerous, are you running away from exciting but risky situations?

Feelings

Another approach you can try is to focus on how you feel about the images, characters, or plot of your dream. How do you feel at different times in the dream? Do those feelings relate to some experience in your everyday life?

Suppose you dream of meeting a beautiful child on the road. The child has blond hair, blue eyes, and a wonderful smile. It stands there beaming at you, and then the dream ends. If you tell someone about that dream, he might say, "Oh, that means that you are discovering a beautiful part of yourself, a part of your inner child." But what if when you see that child on the road you have a sense of dread and foreboding? In that case, the dream may be telling you that looks can be deceiving and you need to see below the surface of people around you.

Plot

You might also ask yourself if the plot of your dream reminds you of any situation in your life. If you dream that you are the victim of an alien conspiracy to take over your house, is there some situation where you feel someone is plotting against you? Do you feel that a co-worker is trying to get your job? Do you feel that someone is interested in your girlfriend or wife and trying to take her away from you? Do you feel that your brother is always trying to turn your mother against you? If so, does the dream have any message for you about that situation? If not, do you have a tendency to be distrustful and paranoid?

Role Playing

Another approach to experiment with is the Gestalt technique of playing each of the images and characters in your dream. If you dream that you climb a mountain and find a flower, and when you pick the flower you're able to fly, you can first be you in the dream. How does it feel to climb the mountain, find the flower, and discover that you can fly? Then you can play the role of the mountain. Who are you and how do you feel about the flower and the person climbing

you? Last, you can be the flower. How do you feel about this person who has come to pick you? Have you been waiting for just this person to come, or can anyone come? Why are you so magical that you make people fly?

Intuition

Finally, you can forget all about particular techniques and just tune in to your intuition. Alfred Adler found that intuition can be one of the best ways to understand yourself. Try putting your questions about a dream aside for a while, and come back to the dream later after you've relaxed and forgotten about it. If all else fails, you can ask your unconscious to give you the message of a dream in another way, by using the lucid dreaming and dream incubation techniques discussed in Chapters 3–5.

COMMON THEMES

There are themes in dreams that many people share, like being chased, falling, and flying. It's important to remember that even though people may have similar dreams, those dreams don't necessarily mean the same thing. In fact, it's very unlikely that they do. So beware of books or interpreters that tell you a dream of exploring a house means finding a new part of yourself or a dream of being chased means you need to deal with your own aggression. What a dream means depends on you, what is happening in you at the time, the associations you make with events in the dream, and how you feel about them.

Here are some of the most common dream themes:

Being Chased

You might be chased by something or someone in your dream, perhaps a lion, a bear, a gangster, a Nazi. How you feel about what is chasing you and what happens in the chase tells you a lot about the meaning of this kind of dream. The standard interpretation of a chase dream is that you are anxious or afraid of some danger in your life. A chase dream might mean that, but it might also mean that you are running away from something you don't really want to run from. If you're afraid of committing yourself to a relationship, what is chasing you might be your idea about being tied down. This is something you are fearful about, but it isn't a real danger in your life.

You can also get information about a chase dream by asking what would happen to you if you were caught. Would a Nazi kill you, put you in a concentration camp? Would a bear eat you, maul you, knock you down, play with you? You may not know what is intended but feel terrified that something bad is going to happen.

All of this reflection can help you understand the nature of what is "after" you in your life, and whether there is a real danger to you or whether you are misunderstanding a situation.

Falling

Another common type of dream that is usually considered an anxiety dream is the dream of falling. Freud, of course, thought that falling dreams meant the dreamers were considering giving in to a sexual urge. Adler thought they meant that the dreamers were afraid of losing status. There is also a folk belief that the dreamer will die if he or she doesn't wake up before hitting the ground. This isn't true, but dreamers often do wake up with a jerk caused by muscle contraction.

The meaning of a falling dream, like that of every other kind of dream, depends on the dreamer. Falling in your dream might mean that you are afraid of losing something or failing in something. We use the expression "falling on your face," to mean failure. Falling could also be about losing control. Perhaps you feel something in your life is out of control. That might be a part of your own personality, a family member, or your job. Have you spread yourself so thin that you don't feel you are on solid ground anymore? Or falling could mean that you are feeling insecure, that there are pitfalls all around you and you might step into one at any moment.

Teeth

Dreams about teeth falling out, crumbling, or breaking are very common. The meaning of such a dream depends on what teeth signify to you and the situation of your dream. If teeth make you think of physical attractiveness, then a dream of crumbling teeth may mean that you're worried about your physical appearance, perhaps feeling unattractive. If you associate teeth with personal appearance, and not just attractiveness, your teeth falling out may mean that you or someone else is pretending to be what you or they are not. If teeth make you think of biting, your teeth

falling out could mean that you should stop making biting and hurtful comments to people. We speak of pulling people's or animals' teeth and mean making them harmless. If you associate teeth with power, then crumbling teeth might indicate a loss of power.

Failing Examinations

Dreams about school and examinations are also common, probably because most of us have spent a large part of our lives in school, often preparing for or taking examinations. There is possibly more variation in school and examination dreams than in other common dream themes. Some dreamers are afraid of failing an examination or have difficulty taking tests. The exams may be illegible, in another language, melt while the dreamer is trying to read them, or be in some other way impossible to understand.

If you are worried about failing an examination, you are focused on the possibility of failure. In the dream you might have studied but still be afraid of failing. You might have forgotten to study and be sure you'll fail as a result, or you may have forgotten about the class. If your dream concerns an examination that you can't read or decipher, it is more likely about your feeling that you are being judged or about your potential for competing. Maybe you feel that you are being judged by unfair criteria.

Being Naked

Finding yourself naked in public is another fairly common theme in dreams. Its meaning has a lot to do with how you feel in the dream. Are you embarrassed, horrified, amused, or relaxed? Are you completely naked or partially clothed? If you are partially clothed, what associations do you have with the clothes that are missing? Dreams of nudity are common and perfectly healthy. The state of being naked is completely natural, like the expression "naked as the day you were born," and nakedness may symbolize a state of simple naturalness.

Exploring Rooms

Another common dream involves exploring rooms in a house. Sometimes the house is one you know and the rooms are ones you didn't know were there. Sometimes you're exploring in an unfamiliar building. Sometimes the rooms need work, but you can see their potential. This is usually a pleasant dream of discovery.

Probably the most common explanation of these dreams is that you are finding a new part of yourself. This may or may not be true. The dream usually seems to be about discovering something, but whether it's an unknown dimension of yourself, resources to start a new business, or unknown dimensions of someone you know will depend on you and what's happening in your life.

Flying

Flying dreams are often described in dream manuals as positive, dreams of joy and exhilaration. Sometimes these dreams are pleasant, with the dreamer soaring high and feeling free, but sometimes they are less pleasant. Sometimes the dreamer is afraid of falling or is unable to get off the ground, stay in the air, or control the flight. All of this is important in understanding what the dream means to you.

The presence and behavior of other characters in a flying dream can also give you important information. Are you the only one who can fly? Are you flying over your family, friends, or co-workers while they look on in amazement? This might mean that you feel superior to them, that they look up to you, or that you have gained a new perspective on them. It all depends on how they seem to feel about you and how you feel about them in the dream.

Being with Celebrities

It is quite ordinary to dream about celebrities. Many people also dream about fictional characters. For example, after the enormous success of the Harry Potter books, both children and adults began to dream that they met or were the characters in the stories. Harry Potter is an orphan who is abused by his aunt and uncle and bullied by his cousin. Suddenly he discovers that he has enormous power: He is a wizard, and he has already defeated the most evil wizard of all time. A dream that you are Harry Potter can be about overcoming adversity, discovering your power, becoming special, or confronting evil. It can also be about having an adventure or starting a new life.

Knowing which dreams contain common themes can help us realize that our seemingly very strange dreams aren't unusual or abnormal. At the same time, it's important to remember that every dream is unique and themes or story lines in dreams don't have standard meanings.

WHAT DOES IT MEAN?

The mystic Edgar Cayce wisely once said that we must interpret the dreamer and not just the dream. The images and characters in your dreams relate to you and the way you communicate with yourself. Most of your dreams will not be based on the common themes we've discussed. They will be scenes and scenarios unique to you. To find the meaning of your dreams, there are several points in the dreams to consider.

People

There is a dispute about whether characters in your dreams are really characters in your life or aspects of your own personality. We mentioned this in the discussion of Gestalt therapy in Chapter 7. The fact is that your unconscious can do anything it wants; it isn't limited by anyone's theories of dreams. Characters in your dreams can be other people in your life, parts of your own psyche, both outside characters and parts of yourself, animals you know, plants, or inanimate objects you have some kind of relationship with, like your car or computer. There is no limit to the ways your unconscious can choose to communicate with you. You will need to discover your own dreaming style.

A character in your dream may not symbolize the person the character seems to be. For example, if you dream about your father, the dream might really be about someone else in your life who has some characteristic of your father or who relates to you as your father did. If you had a loving and supportive relationship with your father, the dream might be about someone who is loving and supportive to you. If your father was authoritarian and you were a little frightened of him, the dream may be about how you're handling personal power. The role of the father might also represent something to you, like the person who provides you with material things. Of course, it's also possible that a dream about your father is actually a message about your relationship with your father.

Animals

Many dream dictionaries and interpretation guides give lists of meanings for animals met in one's dreams. The reality is that the meaning of meeting an animal in your dreams depends on your relationship with that animal or with animals in general.

If you don't like cats or you're extremely allergic to them, the experience of meeting one in your dreams

will be very different from the experience of someone who loves cats. If you're afraid of cats and you dream that a cat moves into your house and won't leave, this will not be a pleasant dream. It may mean you feel threatened or encroached upon in some aspect of your life. For a cat lover, the same dream scenario would probably be very pleasant. Having a new cat come to live with you might indicate a gift or a benign presence. If you think of cats as female, the cat might represent some feminine aspect, as many dream books say, but if you are familiar with tomcats, a cat might relate to some masculine influence in your life.

Perspective

You will also want to pay attention to your perspective as a character in your dreams. Are you in the dream, actually experiencing what's happening? Is a bear chasing you, and all you're aware of is your terror and how fast you can run away? Are you watching the dream like a movie viewer? Are you in the dream but watching it from the outside at the same time? Your perspective on the dream may indicate how you feel about the situation involved. Are you caught up in your role? Are you detached, maybe too detached?

Location

There is an old joke that the three most important things to consider in a real estate deal are location, location, and location. To a certain extent we can say the same thing about a dream. While the characters and plot are important, the location of the dream is often extremely important as well. Location may give us the clue about what the dream means for our everyday lives. Dreams about the workplace, home, childhood haunts, or school, can give us important and valuable clues. If a dream happens in Grandma's house and you always felt happy and loved when you visited her, that sense of happiness might be an important part of the message of your dream.

Location is revealing even when the place of the dream isn't familiar to you. If your dream occurs in a desert, and you think of a desert as a barren place where there isn't enough water, then the dream may relate to a part of you or of your life that feels barren, uncared for, or thirsty. If you love deserts and think of them as beautiful and fascinating places, the dream will have a very different meaning. If you love to walk on beaches, are a dedicated boogie boarder, or are terrified of drowning, the ocean in your dream will have very

dreamfinder

different meanings. Deserts or oceans might also have symbolic meanings for you that have nothing to do with your feelings about actual deserts or oceans. If you think of the ocean as the womb of Gaia, the Earth Mother, then your unconscious may use that symbolism in your dreams.

Weather and Natural Elements

Like animals, weather and seasons of the year have strong emotional associations for us. Some people hate cold weather and choose to live in Florida, Palm Springs, or L.A. Others love skiing, skating, snow-boarding, and drinking hot chocolate in front of the fire. Obviously these people will have very different emotional associations with a dream that takes place in the snow or in an isolated, cold location.

For virtually all of us, spring has a different feeling than winter, and fall has a different feeling than summer. We all have our favorite seasons and our ideas and feelings about them. A dream that takes place in spring may be a code for whatever you think spring is: a new beginning, warm and sunny, full of flowers, a thawing of the winter freeze. A person living in California doesn't have the same images of spring that a person living in Alaska has. Learn to pay attention to the weather and the seasons in your dreams and see what information they give you.

Violent weather events and other natural disasters are also highly emotional. Tidal waves, earthquakes, volcanic eruptions, storms at sea, tornadoes, hurricanes, and thunder and lightning storms, all affect us. If there's a major weather or natural event in your dream, see what that says to you.

Directions

Directions in a dream can sometimes be significant, particularly since our unconscious minds seem to enjoy wordplays. For example, the element of a dream that is "above" could be superior, in charge, in power, unconcerned, or have progressed beyond something. A person or object can be above by flying, levitating, or moving in some apparatus like a plane or balloon, or it can be taller or be standing on something, like a building or mountain. You may be able to figure out what this position means by tuning in to the character or other element that is above the rest and seeing if it feels proud, superior, disdainful, kind, and so on.

Other directions—like forward, in front of, backward, behind, to the right, to the left—also have strong meanings. If some element of your dream is backward, what does that mean to you? Remembering that the unconscious mind can play word games, if you dream that someone is sitting on a chair that is backward, this might indicate that you think that character or the person the character represents is backward or not too intelligent. Or it might mean that you think the person is dishonest.

Things

We are more personally attached to some material things than to others, and these can become quite strong symbols for our dreams. If a guy really loves his car and dreams that someone intentionally scratches it, the dream may be about a feeling of being personally attacked. He may be so identified with his car that it symbolizes an extension of himself. Many of us have other associations with cars that can also be symbolic. What association do you have with a bright red sports car, a rusted pickup with a gun rack, a sports utility vehicle, or an old VW bug with flowers painted on it?

Computers, like cars, evoke a lot of emotions, including love, excitement, envy, frustration, hatred, fear, and dread. If you've never used a computer in your life, but feel like they're taking over the world and spying on your every move, a computer in your dream would be fairly ominous. If you are afraid that your job is going to be computerized and you will become obsolete, a dream about a computer in your workplace will probably be an anxiety dream.

The Human Body

Our bodies are obviously very important to us and also have highly emotional associations. People have every imaginable dream about the human body, from death to dismemberment and injury. They dream about the body enlarging, shrinking, or falling apart. If you dream about someone being dismembered and you don't feel horrified, the dream is most likely not about physical dismemberment but about some metaphorical dismemberment.

We often have strong emotional associations with parts of the body as well. The head may be associated with the intellect, blood with injury, and feet with travel. If blood horrifies you, your unconscious may spread it around in your dream when the message is, Watch out! By contrast, if you think of blood as the stream that brings oxygen to every cell in your body, it may symbolize the live force or river of life. Dreaming about your feet may mean that you feel it's time to move on, or that you need to stand up for yourself. Being buried may be a symbol of being over-whelmed or of becoming unconscious. If you have a fear of being buried alive, a dream of being buried might mean you are feeling suffocated in some aspect of your life. If someone else is being buried in your dream, ask yourself if you are suffocating that person, or is that person going unconscious to avoid engaging with you?

The emotions we have associated with the body make it a very good source of symbols. Don't be too concerned if your dreams are about strange things happening to bodies. They probably don't mean that you're about to become an ax murderer. They most likely mean that your unconscious finds the body a rich source of symbol. If you don't like the symbols your unconscious is using, you can always ask it to use others. You may be surprised at how cooperative it can be.

Clothing

If you don't care much about clothes in your everyday life, chances are that you won't very often notice clothes in your dreams. But clothes, like cars, have strong associations for us. What do you think about a guy wearing a three-piece suit, a polyester leisure suit, several gold chains, baggy shorts and a tank top, or dirty jeans and a leather jacket? We make a lot of assumptions about people based on the clothes they're wearing. We decide whether we can trust them, whether they're dangerous, whether we would like them, and whether they're like us or different. If you realize someone is following you in your dream, notice how the person is dressed. What does that tell you? Is this person dangerous to you?

The clothes you are wearing in your dream also tell you a lot. Are you dressed appropriately for the situation? If you find yourself at a formal ball dressed in jeans and an old sweatshirt, you are probably getting a message about not fitting in or about a fear that you don't fit in. If you are dressed in clothes from another era or place, what associations do those have for you? Are you dressed in knight's armor, an elegant gown, or peasant clothes? How do you feel about that?

Sex

Sigmund Freud may have gone overboard in assuming everything in dreams has to do with sex, but that doesn't mean sex isn't in our dreams. Sex is a big part of our lives and our intimacy. Something that important is bound to come into our dreams. It isn't surprising that a controversy similar to the one about whether characters in our dreams symbolize others or parts of ourselves has arisen about sexual images in our dreams. Some argue that the unconscious is above physical concerns, and sexual dreams are always about internal intercourse and intimacy with ourselves.

Most people would say that sex in their dreams is sometimes just about sex. We dream about our bodies and our emotions, not just our psychological lives. But sex in a dream might not have the literal meaning that first appears. For example, one man whose wife had gone through a difficult time had relied on his step-daughter to help him keep the family together. Later he was upset to find that he was dreaming of having sex with both his wife and his stepdaughter. This dream might not have meant that he was actually interested in having sex with his stepdaughter. It may simply have meant that his stepdaughter had taken on part of the role of wife in the family, a role characterized by having sex with the husband.

We may also dream of having sex with unexpected or inappropriate people, such as people we dislike or distrust, or an ex-spouse. One man was horrified to find that he was in bed with his ex-wife in his dream. It took some time to realize that the new woman he was dating was very much like his ex-wife. The dream wasn't about a desire to sleep with his ex-wife; it was about the way he was refusing to see the traits in his new girlfriend that had led to his divorce. Being "in bed" with someone can also mean conspiring with her or compromising by working with him. It's important to determine whether dreams that use sexual imagery are really about sex.

Of course, sometimes dreams with sexual imagery really are about sexual attraction. Sometimes we don't want to admit we are sexually attracted to someone because we don't want to act on that attraction. When that happens, sexual images may appear in our dreams. If we realize the sexual attraction is a perfectly natural thing and that we have no need to act it out if it isn't appropriate, then admitting to sexual attraction is not a problem. A man who finds a budding young girl sexu-

ally attractive is not abnormal, but a man who acts on that attraction is another matter. Our dreams can help us understand what our sexual attractions really are.

We will get the most out of our dream work if we can relax and enjoy it. If we don't take the images and metaphors in our dreams too seriously or too literally and put aside our judgments about strangeness and pathology, we can begin to have a really good time digging into our own world of symbol and imagination.

MY DREAM THEMES:
DREAMS THAT MAKE ME CALM, JOYFUL, FRIGHTENED